ONCE UPON A RHYME

IMAGINATION FOR A NEW GENERATION

Southern Scotland
Edited by Sarah Marshall

Young Writers

First published in Great Britain in 2004 by:
Young Writers
Remus House
Coltsfoot Drive
Peterborough
PE2 9JX
Telephone: 01733 890066
Website: www.youngwriters.co.uk

All Rights Reserved

© Copyright Contributors 2004

SB ISBN 1 84460 488 8

Foreword

Young Writers was established in 1991 and has been passionately devoted to the promotion of reading and writing in children and young adults ever since. The quest continues today. Young Writers remains as committed to engendering the fostering of burgeoning poetic and literary talent as ever.

This year's Young Writers competition has proven as vibrant and dynamic as ever and we are delighted to present a showcase of the best poetry from across the UK. Each poem has been carefully selected from a wealth of *Once Upon A Rhyme* entries before ultimately being published in this, our twelfth primary school poetry series.

Once again, we have been supremely impressed by the overall high quality of the entries we have received. The imagination, energy and creativity which has gone into each young writer's entry made choosing the best poems a challenging and often difficult but ultimately hugely rewarding task - the general high standard of the work submitted amply vindicating this opportunity to bring their poetry to a larger appreciative audience.

We sincerely hope you are pleased with our final selection and that you will enjoy *Once Upon A Rhyme Southern Scotland* for many years to come.

Contents

Ayton Primary School
    Ryan Thompson (9)   1
    Julie Wieme (7)   1
    Kathryn Beatt (9)   2
    Michael Moran (8)   2
    Cameron Mitchell (10)   3
    Kyla Smith (7)   3
    Hamish Blair (7)   4
    Becky Hannah Holt (7)   4
    Summer Middlemiss (7)   5
    John Inglis (8)   5
    Rachel Tear (10)   5
    Thomas Minto (10)   6
    Nathan Craig (7)   6
    Kieran Power (10)   6

Bellsquarry Primary School
    Markus Wang (9)   7
    Peter McLagan (9)   7
    Cory Smith (9)   8
    Nina Nesbitt (9)   8
    Amy Murray (9)   9
    Jamie MacDonald (9)   9
    Hayley Miller (9)   10
    Mark Pyper (10)   10
    Hannah Peacock (9)   11
    Scott O'Neill (9)   11
    Jordan Lanni (9)   11
    Amy Docherty (9)   12
    Andrew Phelan (9)   12
    Lewis Alexander (9)   13
    Amy Duncan (9)   13
    Sam Huddart   14
    Andrew Saunders (9)   14
    Alexander Wilson (9)   14
    David Burdon (9)   15
    Jamie Crossan (9)   15
    Daniel Lochhead (8)   15
    Callum Williamson (9)   16

Blackford Brae Project
    Benjamin Hardie (11)   16
    Darren Walker (12)   17

Carsphairn Primary School
    Hannah Blackett (8)   17
    Rebecca Holden (10)   18

Cramond Primary School
    Kit Gilchrist (11)   19

Dalbeattie Primary School
    Natasha Burrows (11)   20
    Aimee Tibbins (11)   20
    Gina Bertolacci (7)   21
    Rebecca Kirk (7)   21
    Jennifer Tapner (7)   22
    Jack Porter (7)   22
    Megan Kirkpatrick (7)   22
    Fern Davidson (10)   23
    Victoria Price (10)   23
    Eloise Cox (11)   24
    Abbie Hill (7)   24
    Sheona Lindsay (11)   25
    Katrina Henderson (11)   25
    Kerri Wilson (11)   26
    Steven Wilson (7)   26
    Hannah Greenway (7)   27
    Jessica Bell (7)   27
    Abbie Charters (11)   28
    Ruth Crichton (6)   28
    Aimee Anderson (11)   29
    Lesley Rae (10)   29

Echline Primary School
    Rowan Hall (9)   30

Elmvale Primary School
    Jennifer Chiu (11)   31
    Philippa Billson (10)   32

Bradey Maxwell (10)	32
Ashleigh Rennie (11)	33
James McCall (11)	33
Kirsti Wallace (10)	34
Amy Buchanan (11)	34
Jamie Walker (11)	35
Brady Graham (11)	35
Stacey Graham (11)	36
Thomas Graham (11)	36
Leanne Little (12)	37
Rachael Carey (11)	37

Howgate Primary School

Abigail Martin (8)	38
Jenny Johnston (8)	38
Martin Swapp (10)	39
Marie McGeachie (9)	39
Caitlin Reid (9)	40
Olivia Bird (8)	40
Amy Steel (8)	41

Humbie Primary School

Douglas McLean (9)	42

Hutton Primary School

Jessica Cotterill (10)	42
Emma Singleton (11)	43
Conor O'Neill (10)	43
Gwen Dupre (10)	43
Kate Jackson (10)	44
Craig Scott (10)	44
Adam Cotterill (9)	45

Kinneil Primary School

Taylor McIntyre & Stephanie Auld (10)	45
Robyn Burns (9)	46

Kirkpatrick Fleming Primary School

Sean Cruikshank (10)	46
Thomas Illingworth (10)	46

Phoebe Lockhart (10)   47
Conor Smith (10)   47
Danielle Story (11)   48
Kirsty Prentice (9)   48
Isabella Graham-Campbell (9)   49
Kirsty Hotchkiss (10)   49
Cameron Lockhart (10)   50
Leanne Postlethwaite (10)   50
Conor Allan (9)   51

Knowepark Primary School
Bryar Mennie (8)   51
Cameron Younger (8)   51
Kieran Challinor (8)   52
Sarah McColm (8)   52
Andrew Anderson (8)   53
Tiffany Duncan (8)   53
Jack Borthwick (8)   54
Alex Carroll (8)   54
Liam Murray (8)   55
Hamish Robinson (8)   55
Mairi Chisholm (8)   55
Shelley McLeish (8)   56
Andrew Nichol (8)   56
Emily Anderson (8)   56
Iona Matheson (8)   57
Alastair Penny (8)   57
Evie Anderson (8)   58
Craig Bruce (8)   58
Caitlin Tait (8)   59
Adam Nichol (8)   59

Letham Primary School
Matthew McEwan (10)   60
Brian Dibben (10)   61
Douglas McAdam (8)   61
Shaun Wilson (10)   62

Locharbriggs Primary School
Jamie Rae (11)   62

Hannah Irving (11)	63
Stacey Cullen (11)	63
Amie Byers (11)	64
Eilidh McRobert (11)	64
Scott Padmore (11)	65
Ryan Learmont (11)	65
John Darren Davidson (11)	66
Jade Aitken (11)	66
Marita Barr (11)	67

Loretto Junior School

Sophie Russell (11)	68
Edward Dudgeon (10)	68
Harry Marriott & Alexander Byers (10)	69
Danielle Walton (10)	69
Megan Selley (10)	70

Murrayburn Primary School

Rebecca Scott (11)	71
Scott McDonald (11)	71
Martin Hickey (11)	72
Kimberley Dunn (11)	73
Nicola Robertson (11)	73
Sara Willis (11)	74
Sara Bavidge (11)	74
Corey Robertson (11)	75
Ryan Lee (10)	75
Katie Flockhart (11)	76
Dale Brown (11)	77
Brian Dudgeon (11)	78
Jamie Proudfoot (11)	78
Jean Welsh (11)	79
Christopher Robertson (11)	79
Vikki Baigrie (11)	80
Amanda Cameron (11)	80

Newington Primary School

Josh Marshall (8)	81
Ryan Ferguson (8)	81
Robbie McWhirter (7)	82

Zoe Harkness (8)	82
Eilidh Wright (8)	83
Laura Allison (8)	84
Logan Creighton (8)	85
Callum Rogerson (8)	86
Shannon Morrin (8)	87

Oxgangs Primary School

Gavin Hogg (10)	87
Nicole Anderson (10)	88
Karen Gibson (10)	89
Melissa Collins (11)	89
Karen Ewing (11)	90
Fraser Robertson (11)	90
Graham Dickson (10)	91
Nick Cross (10)	91
Rachel Laing (9)	92
Adjana Mason (11)	93
Vikki Brash (11)	93
David Sivewright (11)	93
Paula Campbell (7)	94
Claire Anderson (7)	94
Iain Mackay (7)	95
Rebecca Cork (7)	95
Rachael Erskine (7)	95
Amanda Wilson (7)	96
Adam Murphy (7)	96
Struan Sloan (7)	96
Briony O'Keefe (9)	97
Adam Weir (9)	97
Nadia Hussain (9)	98
Yasmin Rasul (9)	98
Alex Cork (11)	99
Emily Youngs (7)	99
Nicola Peat (10)	100
Carly Burnett (9)	101
Scott Wilson (12)	101
Sarah Hunter (10)	102
Leigh Innes (7)	102
Eleanor Campbell (10)	103
Molly Meikle (7)	103

Grant Clark (11) — 104
Carrie Smith (11) — 104
Euan Ballantyne (11) — 105
Natty Clark (7) — 105
Kyle Adamson (10) — 106

Palnackle Primary School
Emily Mann (10) — 106
Molly Irving (10) — 107
Lucy Niven — 108
Tom Niven (9) — 108
Fraser Firth (8) — 108
Chloe Ellis (11) — 109

Sanquhar Primary School
Callum Park (10) — 109
Isabel Gordon (10) — 110
Brenna Aston (10) — 111
Ben Waugh (10) — 112
Leigh Clark (10) — 112
Colin Baird (10) — 113
Coral Anderson (10) — 113
Neil Moffat (10) — 114
Brendan Moore (10) — 115
Rachel Wilson (10) — 115

St Joseph's RC Primary School, Stranraer
Kieran McCusker — 116
Jade McCulloch (8) — 116
Stacy Paterson (10) — 116
Lauren Lowe (9) — 117
Amber Feeney (7) — 117
Elliot Monaghan (7) — 117
Heather Corrigan (9) — 118
Kiera Hilton (7) — 118
Matthew Love (8) — 118
Rachel Drysdale (8) — 119
Gregor Feeney (9) — 119
Fergus Lochhead (8) — 119
Chelsea Westran (9) — 120

Jennifer McCusker (9)	120
Poppy Arkless (9)	121
Kyle McCulloch (10)	121
Samantha Henderson (10)	122
Jeri-Ann Mulligan (10)	122
Robert Mackenzie (10)	123
Shannan Corrigan (11)	124
Iona Donnelly (11)	124
Karina McCusker (10)	125
Gina Soriani (11)	125

St Mary's Music School, Edinburgh

Andrew Bull (10)	126
Kieran Baker (9)	127
Caitlin Spencer (10)	127
Alice Burn (11)	128
Katherine Carr (9)	129

St Mary's RC Primary School, Bonnyrigg

Chiara Margiotta (8)	129
Shaun Muir (8)	130
Paul Brogan (8)	130
Ashleigh MacFeate (8)	131
Adriane Napa (8)	131
Gemma Smith (8)	132
Rosie Jones (8)	132
Hannah Brosnan (8)	133
Erin Devine (8)	133
Rachael Douglas (8)	134
Diana McLaren (8)	134
Clara Fraser (8)	135
Islay Coppola (8)	135
Hayley Wilson (8)	135
Erin Brolly (8)	136
Carly Gulland (8)	136
Kyle Wilson (8)	137
Sean Thomson (8)	137
Shannon McAra (8)	138
Mark Kean (8)	138

Steven Gilmour (8)	139
Daniel Morrison (8)	139
Stewart Brown (8)	140

Stobhill Primary School

Natasha Cumming (8)	140
Sean McColm (8)	141
Kimberley Rice (8)	141
Kyle Fleming (8)	142
Natalie Cumming (8)	142
Chloe Birrell (8)	143
Amy Cornwall (8)	143
Glenn Ross (8)	144

The Mary Erskine & Stewart's Melville Junior School

Sophie Graham (9)	144
Holly Drummond (9)	145
Jessica Findlay (9)	146

Westruther Primary School

Callum Airlie (8)	147
James Conington (8)	148
Elizabeth Wilson (8)	148
Drew Airlie (10)	149
Suzan Reshad (11)	149
Joanna Wilson (8)	150
Holly Reshad (9)	150
Jennifer Smith (11)	151
Oliver Muir (11)	152
Kathleen Long (10)	152

Whitdale Primary School

Scott Kempik (9)	153
Harris Loureiro (9)	153
Callum Millar (9)	154
Eva Leslie (9)	154
Connor McGonigal (9)	155
Sophie Renwick (9)	155
April Penman (9)	156
Andrew Easton (9)	156

Aaron Brown (10) 157
Megan Brady (9) 158
Jonathan Hay (9) 158
Lauren Stewart (9) 159
Louise Walker (9) 159
Lauren Wilson (9) 160
Gareth Campbell (10) 160
Tiffany Whiteford (9) 161
Rachel Cunningham (10) 161
Tammy Dickson (10) 162
Patrick Thornton (10) 162
Aimee Douglas (10) 163
Vicky Christie (10) 163
Sarah McNeill (10) 164
Jasmyn Leigh Crowden (9) 165
Claire Longridge (10) 166
Aimee McMahon (10) 166
Jade Ford (10) 167
Caitlin Stone (8) 167
Jason Cleland (8) 168
Jemma White (8) 168
Alistair Brown (8) 169
Kirsty Jack (8) 169
Lauren Kerr (9) 169
Sarah Cochrane (8) 170
Debbie Cuthbert (8) 170
Lauren Bonnar & Heather Weir (8) 170
Jack Compton (8) 171
Lewis Perry (8) 171
Ryan Douglas (8) 171
Darcey O'Rourke (8) 172

Woodburn Primary School
Allan Thomson (11) 172
Ryan Dempster (11) 173
Alisha Allen (11) 173
Samantha Howie (11) 174
Sammi Kelly (11) 174
Laura Haining (11) 175

Paul Hart (11)	176
William Baxter (11)	176
Iesha Steele (11)	177
Dean Watson (11)	178

The Poems

Deserted

No leaves on the trees,
A dirty old bridge,
A light orange sky,
A golden river,
Leaves cover up the ground,
No animals.
Brown, orange and yellow leaves,
An old deserted house,
A rusty chimney,
No fish in the rivers.
Very old trees,
A stone bridge,
A shiny sky,
Water flowing fast,
Animals hibernating for the winter,
Crumpled-up leaves.

Ryan Thompson (9)
Ayton Primary School

Poppies

Poppies are red,
A lovely bright colour,
They grow in the fields,
The red means blood,
Blood from the men who were fighting,
Buried in the Flanders Field in France,
The black of the poppy makes people feel sad
But I think poppies are lovely.

Julie Wieme (7)
Ayton Primary School

The Jungle

One enormous dazzling sun,
One big blue sky,
Soft bouncy clouds.

Big soft green leaves,
Huge long bamboo shoots,
Enormous razor-sharp leaves,
Huge bulky attractive plants,
Big tall leaves surrounding
Beautifully scented flowers.

Night-flying bats,
Hairy lions,
Big wild animals,
Groups of hairy apes,
Big fierce tiger,
Talking parrots,
Branch-hanging sloths.

Soft white fog,
Hot days and cold nights,
Soft falling rain.

Kathryn Beatt (9)
Ayton Primary School

Poppies

Red are the poppies,
Growing in the fields,
Over the dead bodies,
It helps you remember
The people of the war,
Bright colours that you can see.

Michael Moran (8)
Ayton Primary School

The Jungle

Careful creeping creatures,
Slow slithering snakes,
Big fierce animals,
Noisy parrots,
Heavy rain,
Damp nights,
Wet and windy,
Misty mornings,
Big colourful plants,
Bright light,
Pitch-black,
Hot days,
Cold.

Cameron Mitchell (10)
Ayton Primary School

Flanders Fields

L onely land,
A ir blows,
N astiness,
D eath,
E erie,
R unning men,
S torms of feet,

F ields,
I ce-cold mornings,
E nemies,
L it lanterns,
D eadly men,
S unny days.

Kyla Smith (7)
Ayton Primary School

An Old Deserted House

An old deserted house
Birds leaving for warmer countries
Robins come to say hello
Twisted trees climbing up to the sky
Leaves all different colours
Yellow, brown and orange
Falling down branches
Tumbling bridge falling down
Water flowing lazily along
Cold nights and days
Ivy hanging from the house
Tumbling down house
It starts to rain and snow
Squirrels gather nuts ready for winter
No one around.

Hamish Blair (7)
Ayton Primary School

The Old House

Old crumbling bridges
tower over the house.
A glowing moon above the trees
in a dark black sky.
Crunchy leaves upon the ground.
Autumn light flies through
the branches, dazzling the world.
The river flows slowly.
A broken fence of rusty metal
lies on the ground.

Becky Hannah Holt (7)
Ayton Primary School

Poppies

Poppies are red because it stands for blood
Black stands for death,
Flanders Field had lots and lots of poppies,
You could hardly see them,
There was too much mist,
People died in Flanders Field,
No one saw them ever again.

Summer Middlemiss (7)
Ayton Primary School

The Creator

God made Adam and God made Eve,
They lived in a house across the seas,
They cared for the animals - they sang them songs,
Until night came they lived happily on,
They slept in a bed made of rock and straw,
Some leaves for a cover and a pillow kept them warm.

John Inglis (8)
Ayton Primary School

Spring Haikus

Daffodils are out,
Lambs jump on the bales and play,
Lambs are here so soon.

Snowdrops are snow white,
Daffodils are tall not small,
Ducks are swimming fast.

Rachel Tear (10)
Ayton Primary School

Spring Haikus

Lambs are being born
Rabbits are hopping about
Buds are growing fast

Calves are warm in spring
Ducks are swimming in the pond
Tulips are purple

Sheep are having lambs
Leaves on trees are growing fast
Snowdrops grow in spring.

Thomas Minto (10)
Ayton Primary School

An Old Wood

An old brick bridge,
A slow muddy river,
Leaves falling lightly on the water,
Lots of trees swaying in the wind,
Trees are falling,
Crunchy leaves on the ground,
The house is deserted,
Windows are smashed.

Nathan Craig (7)
Ayton Primary School

Spring Haikus

Flowers are growing,
Yesterday it stopped snowing,
Spring is coming soon.

Sheep have now been sheared,
No snow today it looks weird,
Spring is here at last.

Kieran Power (10)
Ayton Primary School

Oresakelesi

The Oresakelesi is a funny beast
With its eight legs
It likes to wander
Wander through the streets at night
And frighten every living thing!

They go intae their wee hooses
And nae come out agen!

Because of the ugly beast
That roams the streets agen!

Markus Wang (9)
Bellsquarry Primary School

Cobparsharn

The Cobparsharn has the head of a piranha,
A cobra's neck too,
A giant shark's body,
With a leopard's tail too.
All this together makes him look strange,
Everyone calls him the monster of the sea,
But believe me,
He wouldn't hurt a flea,
Because he's a vegetarian
And he's my best friend.

Peter McLagan (9)
Bellsquarry Primary School

The Jellongeckoon

The Jellongeckoon is a funny beast
it doesn't look the same
it's got a jellyfish as a head
it can't see a thing

It's got the body of a Gecko
it can stick to things on end
but it could never replace
the next body part

Next is a baboon's legs
they are as blue as the sea
people can see these legs from miles around
even the clouds can see them

Last of all is the lion's tail
it wags its tail when it's happy
it stops wagging if the Jellongeckoon is sad

Don't get in this beast's bad books
or he'll eat you as fast as he can!

Cory Smith (9)
Bellsquarry Primary School

The Catelephleoptrou

The Catelephleoptrou has a head of an elephant,
It has a body of a cat and a leopard,
The Catelephleoptrou is also half trout.

The Catelephleoptrou would never shout,
He only eats grass and weed,
Also lives under the sea, but will never look like me.

Nina Nesbitt (9)
Bellsquarry Primary School

Atolphinarkerfly

My name is Atolphinarkerfly
And I have wings from a butterfly
That are pink with spots

A body like a shark to dive
Beneath the sea
And a tail like a dolphin
To help me swim fast

And last of all a face of a cat
So I can see in the dark
And I love to dive in the sea.

Amy Murray (9)
Bellsquarry Primary School

Moarkcobeag

The Moarkcobeag is a funny beast,
It can fly very high,
It has the head of a snake,
The body of a shark,
The wings of an eagle
And the legs and arms of a Komodo Dragon,
It's huge,
It's scary,
It's the Moarkcobeag!
They exist all over the world,
Have you seen one?

Jamie MacDonald (9)
Bellsquarry Primary School

The Pusturionfly

The Pusturionfly has the legs of an octopus,
The body of a turtle
And the wings of a butterfly,
He is one of a kind
And has no friends,
Apart from one who will be there to the end.
His friend is a dragon and is very sweet,
They both love good things to eat,
For supper they have ham and bread,
Then they go up to bed.

Hayley Miller (9)
Bellsquarry Primary School

Sharabanhaal

The head of a piranha
The pincers and legs of a crab
The body of a shark
And the tail of an eel
Everyone fears it, no one has seen it
It can smash through a rock like scissors and paper
It destroys everything in its way
I'll catch it someday.

Mark Pyper (10)
Bellsquarry Primary School

The Allidoglamerbuff

The Allidoglamerbuff is a big hairy thing,
He runs as fast as a jet
And has a horn on top of his head.
He swooshes his tail like a train,
His back legs have sharp claws like a dragon,
He is running back to his herd,
He is having something to eat,
He is frightening all the people in the street,
And roams all the world again forever.

Hannah Peacock (9)
Bellsquarry Primary School

Killpenguffader

The Killpenguffader is a funny beast
With the head of a buffalo
A body of a whale
The legs of a spider
And the feet of a penguin
People come to see this magic beast.

Scott O'Neill (9)
Bellsquarry Primary School

Rillaguinboonopus

It has got eight tentacles,
The head of a gorilla,
It has penguin feet,
The body of a gorilla,
It catches a fish with a beak,
The tail helps it swing from tree to tree.

Jordan Lanni (9)
Bellsquarry Primary School

The Zeraffeoctoat

The Zeraffeoctoat has the head of a cat,
The tail of a zebra,
The legs of an octopus
And the neck of a giraffe.
Everyone stares at the sight of it,
It plods along reaching for food,
Nobody knows if it's a male or female,
I take pictures for the newspaper,
My mum takes pictures to take to her work,
This thing can be a lot of trouble
Because it needs a lot of water,
This great big beast belongs to me,
Nobody will take him away.

Amy Docherty (9)
Bellsquarry Primary School

The Girant Shagon

The Girant Shagon is an elephant,
Giraffe, shark and a dragon,
He has a head like a dog,
He has a tail like an alien,
A wing like a chicken,
But always lives in a cave.

Andrew Phelan (9)
Bellsquarry Primary School

The Sucker Squeezer

The Sucker Squeezer is a funny beast
Snake as either arm or leg,
The Sucker Squeezer is an empire penguin,
A baboon, a snake and elephant all together.

When the wind blows to cool the beast
It just flaps its hair
And starts a hurricane.

The Sucker Squeezer is a guard,
When an enemy comes near
It just sucks him over and squeezes him.

Lewis Alexander (9)
Bellsquarry Primary School

Shahoratig

A face of a cat,
A tail of a shark,
The legs of a horse,
The body of a pig,
Nobody knows if it is a female or a male,
Everybody is scared of it,
It is a fast runner,
It has been in the newspaper five times
And people come to take pictures of it,
It is very hard to look after.

Amy Duncan (9)
Bellsquarry Primary School

Octobooneelebuff

A buffalo's head,
An elephant's trunk,
An octopus' legs
And a baboon's bottom.
It's a strange creature,
But it wouldn't hurt a fly.
It's not one of the fastest creatures around,
It travels at 1 mile per hour.

Sam Huddart
Bellsquarry Primary School

Cheemodoganion

The Cheemodoganion
has the tail and arms of a Komodo dragon
The wings and body of a peregrine falcon
Feet of a cheetah
A lion's head
He soars through the sky
Runs faster than a cheetah
And has a golden mane
At night he goes back to Cheemodo Island.

Andrew Saunders (9)
Bellsquarry Primary School

The Komosharoctoeagle

The Komosharoctoeagle is a legendary beast
Two heads of a komodo dragon and eagle
Eight long tentacles from an octopus
And a long tail of a shark
It comes from a distant land called Como Island
Breathes fire like a star
It's a strange beast in the world
It's my best friend.

Alexander Wilson (9)
Bellsquarry Primary School

The Legendary Snabchabguin

The Snabchabguin has the head of a penguin,
The body of a chameleon,
The legs and nippers of a crab,
The tail of a snake,
The legend says whoever goes near it will be chopped in half.

People come from all around the world to worship it,
It feeds on fish with its long neck to reach its prey,
Its legs are good for escaping its enemies.

David Burdon (9)
Bellsquarry Primary School

The Ducrocsharab

The Ducrocsharab is an underwater beast,
That likes to have a feast.
It has the jaws of a crocodile,
The claws of a crab,
It swims underwater with the tail and fins of a shark,
It's got the webbed feet of a duck to zoom across the surface,
But every so often it goes down to the murky black Scarab Cave.

Jamie Crossan (9)
Bellsquarry Primary School

The Octoheoiphish

The Octoheoiphish is half octopus,
Horse, elephant and fish.

It swims like a fish,
Runs like a horse,
As loud as an elephant,
A face like an octopus.

Daniel Lochhead (8)
Bellsquarry Primary School

The Octophantigra

The Octophantigra is a big beast,
He is as fat as a pig and very lazy,
Eight legs sticking out of his head,
It never lays eggs but maybe it was a fossil
And came back from the dead
And is my friend.

Callum Williamson (9)
Bellsquarry Primary School

The Gold Cat

T he gold cat is a magical creature
H e who finds it gets three wishes
E asier said than done

G reat people have searched
O n every continent
L ong have they travelled
D own hills, up mountains

C lever, oh so clever he is
A nd no one has lived
T o tell the tale.

Benjamin Hardie (11)
Blackford Brae Project

The Time Machine

Press the red button, off we go
Back in time to a land long ago
It was different, the cars were old
Slaves were bought and sold
The machine was going back in time
I saw a dinosaur, it looked fine
I was scared and ran away
Back in time to find another day

Press the red button, off we go
Back in time to a land long ago
I saw my granddad in the war
He said goodbye at the door
Sad to see him go away
And never come back another day
With a tear in my eye
I go home for some mince pie.

Darren Walker (12)
Blackford Brae Project

The Best Pet

My hamster's name is Mr Mole
He looks just like a piece of coal
With eyes and ears and two pairs of feet
And every night again we meet
When we do, up he'll jump
And land back on his little rump
Though he's not a rabbit in a hutch
I love him very, very much.

Hannah Blackett (8)
Carsphairn Primary School

The Wind

The wind passes day and night
First it starts off very light

A calm breeze flurries and flutters
As it blows past all the gutters

It rushes around oh so fast
I think that I'm going to be last

It whistles and rattles around in rage
As though it's trapped inside a cage

It howls and roars, it bangs on doors
It rushes around on all the floors

It comes howling past so very fast
It's worse than they said on the weather forecast

A stream of hair hits my cheeks so bare
As I stand to watch and stare

But then again no one knows
If the wind has eyes, ears or even a nose.

Rebecca Holden (10)
Carsphairn Primary School

Feeling Good

Wandering around,
Coughing from all the smoke,
Cramped together,
Up above a grey cloudy sky,
Feeling alone . . .

Seeing open space,
Looking at the brightness,
Small brick buildings,
What a new lightness,
Feeling nervous . . .

Excitement all around,
Meeting Zach in a shop,
Drawing things I see,
Loving my new life,
Feeling up at the top . . .

Going back to London,
Darkness all around,
Holding Trudy in my arms,
Banging noises can be heard,
Feeling sad . . .

Up the road on the bikes,
Salt-on-the-mouth is fine,
Swimming in the big blue sea,
This is the life for me,
Feeling happy . . .

Thinking deeply in my mind,
Down in there what do I find?
Performing in a funny way,
What a very emotional day,
Feeling warm . . .

Kit Gilchrist (11)
Cramond Primary School

The Dentist

I'm going to see the dentist
I'm trembling in the seat
I brushed my teeth this morning
Then had a pile of sweets.

I can't resist the toffees
The sherbet that makes your face shrill
There is only one downside
When he gets out the drill!

He's got all his pointy needles
He creeps along the floor
But before he looks into my mouth
I'm halfway out the door!

Natasha Burrows (11)
Dalbeattie Primary School

Far Away

I know we may be far away
And far apart we are,
But you are near to me
As you are right by my heart.

I know you may be missing me
As I am missing you,
Catch up on all the gossip
And all the things you do.

I know we may be far away
But I'll never ever forget you!

Aimee Tibbins (11)
Dalbeattie Primary School

Autumn Changes

I can see the red squirrel,
It is climbing up a tree.
I can see a hedgehog eating fat,
I can see a tree with red leaves,
I can see the leaves falling off the tree.

I can hear the birds tweeting,
I can hear the leaves crunching,
I can hear a hedgehog sleeping,
I can hear the wind blowing,
I can hear the foxes running,
I can hear you.

Gina Bertolacci (7)
Dalbeattie Primary School

Autumn

Autumn changes all around
Autumn changes on the ground
Autumn changes on the trees
Autumn changes on the leaves
I can see shining conkers
I can see some acorns dropping
Hedgehogs pick up the acorns
Hedgehogs will have food for hibernating.

Rebecca Kirk (7)
Dalbeattie Primary School

Autumn Changes

Can you see the mushroom grow?
Can you see the blackberry show?
Juicy berries for only little me

I can hear a hedgehog rustling in the crunchy leaves
When I step on them
I can hear a bird chirp in the tree.

Jennifer Tapner (7)
Dalbeattie Primary School

Autumn Changes

I can see the squirrel in the trees and the red leaves,
I can see the conkers, they are very smooth
And they have prickly shells.
I can see the birds singing in the trees,
I can hear the birds singing,
The birds are going to migrate,
I can hear the leaves crackle when I stand on them.

Jack Porter (7)
Dalbeattie Primary School

Autumn Changes

Autumn changes on the trees
Autumn changes on the leaves
See the squirrels on the trees
See the juicy brambles on their branches
Hear the leaves rustling up above
I like the wind rustling in the trees.

Megan Kirkpatrick (7)
Dalbeattie Primary School

World's Desires

I can't see the wind
But I can see the snow
Sometimes I wonder
What the world holds

I think someone knows
What the world holds
So I'm going to find them
And learn what must be told

I know the journey will be cold
So I'll take some coal to make a fire
I want to know what is the world's desire.

Fern Davidson (10)
Dalbeattie Primary School

Solo

Hey look there's my pal, Solo
He's the one out there playing polo
He drives his master
He runs even faster
His thanks to him are for the win

The field is soft
Then *whoosh* they're off
He shines in the limelight
He puts up a great fight
His energy soars
When the crowd starts to roar
That's my pal, Solo.

Victoria Price (10)
Dalbeattie Primary School

Miracle Horse!

Ted, Ted, he's the best,
Better than all the rest.
He can jump up really high,
I can nearly touch the sky.

His movements so smooth, he swiftly glides,
As he does what I ask with one tap on his sides.
His coat is so shiny,
His mane is so fair,
This horse of mine is a beauty so rare.

Cantering over the sunlit hills,
Trotting smoothly round his field.
Now it is time to say goodnight,
I'll see you again when the sky is light.

This horse is so gorgeous, so loving, so kind,
The most peaceful horse you could ever find.
Watching him galloping around so free,
Glad to know that he loves me.

I'm in my car,
I'm going home.
Leave my horse alone to roam,
Leave him to eat the fresh green grass,
Time for him to rest at last.

Ted's the best there could ever be,
I love Ted, he's the one for me.

Eloise Cox (11)
Dalbeattie Primary School

Autumn Changes

I can see the leaves change red, brown and yellow.
I can see the fungi grow, the fungi feels very smooth.
I can hear the hedgehog rustling amongst the leaves.
I can hear the birds cheep.
I can hear a deer running through the woods.

Abbie Hill (7)
Dalbeattie Primary School

What's Under My Bed?

Shh, it's here, it's under my bed,
It's slimy and green and its name is Fred,
It's furry and old and looks like mould,
Oh please do something with Fred.
I'll suddenly wake up and it will all be a dream,
But what if it isn't? I'll jump up and scream.
He'll climb up the covers and tickle my toes,
Let's just hope he doesn't get my nose.
I've got to be brave and get up and see
What's under my bed and waiting for me,
I finally stand up,
Look under my bed
And realise at last it was all in my head!

Sheona Lindsay (11)
Dalbeattie Primary School

Feelings

Everybody feels different,
Sometimes you can be sad and others happy,
Or sometimes you can even be in-between,
It basically depends on the time,
As I write this poem
I feel proud in who I am
In every single way!

Katrina Henderson (11)
Dalbeattie Primary School

Seaside Poem

I feel
The soft and gentle sand
Which I use to make a sandcastle
The wavy breezy seawater
Which I swim and relax in
The hard sharp rock
Which I sit on to eat my picnic

I see
The boats bobbing up and down on the sea
Little boys and girls fishing in rock pools
Men and women sunbathing
Trying to get a tan

I hear
Babies screaming for their mums and dads
Children screaming because the water is too cold
Girls and boys splashing having fun.

Kerri Wilson (11)
Dalbeattie Primary School

Playing

P laying is fun
L aughing in the sun
A t the park fishing for a shark
Y ou and me stuck in a tree
I magine in a tractor going faster and faster
N obody is naughty calling people names
G reat fun in the park just playing games.

Steven Wilson (7)
Dalbeattie Primary School

Autumn Changes

I can see the red squirrels on a horse chestnut tree.
I can see the red rosehips on the bush.
I can see the hawthorn and it is prickly.
I can see the red and brown leaves.
I can see the acorns on the oak trees.

I can hear the conkers drop on the ground.
I can hear the leaves rustling.
I can hear a hedgehog rustling in the leaves.
I can hear a rabbit jumping in the leaves.
I can hear the birds cheeping in the morning.

Hannah Greenway (7)
Dalbeattie Primary School

Autumn Changes

I can see the brambles ripen.
I can see the acorns on the oak tree.
I can see lots of leaves falling off the tree.
They are all different colours.
I can hear the leaves fall off the tree.
I can hear the hedgehog rustling in the leaves.
I can hear the rabbits jumping and rustling in the leaves.
They are looking for food.

Jessica Bell (7)
Dalbeattie Primary School

I Don't Want To Do My Homework!

I don't want to do my homework!
It's not got to be in for a few days,
I'll do it tomorrow instead Mum,
I'll go out and play today!

I don't want to do my homework!
In fact, I don't have any at all (ha ha!)
I'll bring it home tomorrow Mum,
I'm going out to play ball!

Oh Mum, oh Mum, help me please,
My homework is to be in tomorrow!
I shouldn't have gone out, I shouldn't have footered about,
Oh homework is such sweet sorrow!

Abbie Charters (11)
Dalbeattie Primary School

Autumn Changes

I can see a red squirrel on a chestnut tree
looking for some conkers
I can see the brambles on a bramble bush
And they are so ripe
I can hear the hedgehog rustling in the leaves from the trees
I can hear the rabbits jumping
And rustling in the leaves
And they are looking for some food.

Ruth Crichton (6)
Dalbeattie Primary School

Muffy

Have you seen Muffy?
He is big, white and fluffy,
He jumps and skips,
Cuddles and licks,
Running over hills,
He needs no pills.
A brush and comb
He'll need when he gets home,
Have you got him a bone?
Oh no, he'll moan.
Poor old Muffy,
He's so huffy.

Aimee Anderson (11)
Dalbeattie Primary School

Stars

Sparkling stars twinkling,
Bright stars shining,
Heavenly stars glittering,
Racing through the sky,
So the sun is out, so it's time to say
Goodbye.

Lesley Rae (10)
Dalbeattie Primary School

Deep As The Colours

Darkest of them all,
Black is so parsimonious,
As bleak as it would be,
Frigid like the sea.

Red is like blood, dripping down an arm,
She is so irate.
She nearly always causes harm,
But she is still full of agony.

Like red,
Orange is so hot,
Too hot to be sad,
Though happier than the lot.

Blue breathes fresh air,
Delicate,
He could easily tear,
He is so amicable,
Everyone is his mate.

Envious green,
Oh how he longs to be on top!
He just won't stop,
Always wanting to be seen.

Yellow is bold and bright,
Blinded,
At first sight,
As ponderous as a newborn baby.

Pink is the baby out of all colours,
Cute and cuddly,
But also shy,
She doesn't like it when you say goodbye.

Rowan Hall (9)
Echline Primary School

My Life Is Like The Music

My life is like the music, an everlasting river,
A soft and gentle melody,
Oh my life is like the music for all eternity.

Crescendos like my growing anger, fear and woe, anticipation,
A diminuendo is like a mother's love, sweet, calm and nurturing.

My life is like the music, it's staccato
But I wish for once that it was legato.

The beat of the drum like my thumping heart,
My role in life is a little part.
The chorus of a song so like my family,
There for me repeatedly.

Black and white keys like the night
And the day, gay songs watch children play.

Songs of the winter seasons of the sun,
Watch and listen as the wheel of life will turn.

Angels look down from the heavens,
Their magical notes from the harp weaving around us,
Tendrils sent every direction.

The heart of the music is within me,
With its golden rhythm beating.

My life is like the music,
It's magic honestly,
Put your hand on my heart and hear a melody,
My life is and always will be
Like the music.

Jennifer Chiu (11)
Elmvale Primary School

My Mum And Dad

My mother is the best one yet,
She's the best mum any girl could get!
She's got dark red hair and grass-green eyes
And lovely red lips that are divine.
She's got gorgeous soft skin and wears cool new clothes,
She's funny and joyful, merry and bright!
My mother is the best one yet,
She's the best mum any girl could get!
My dad is the best dad yet!
He's the best dad any girl could get,
He wakes me in the morning to get dressed for school
And gets me there on time,
He tucks me in bed at night,
My dad is the best one yet,
He's the best dad any girl could get!

Philippa Billson (10)
Elmvale Primary School

My Dad

My dad has blue eyes,
My dad has brown hair,
He makes me giggle all the time,
He bumps his head all day long,
Because he is so tall.
My dad gets so bored, so he falls asleep and snores.
He has big feet that when he walks, they bang the floor.
My dad buys me sweets every day,
The sun shines on his eyes and makes them sparkle,
He's only a little bit of hair, he's nearly bald,
You could say he is silly, but he's not, he's funny.

Bradey Maxwell (10)
Elmvale Primary School

Why?

Why is the world round not flat?
Why can cats be grey and black?
Why do babies weep and cry?
Why do people live and die?
Why is the world so colourful and light?
Why does the sun shine down so bright?
Why is the world full of hate and dread?
Why do we sleep in a bed?
Why do we cry and laugh?
Why do we take a bath?
Why at night is it calm and still?
I don't know but I love the world
I think it's brill!

Ashleigh Rennie (11)
Elmvale Primary School

Scary Mary Rap

My name is Scary Mary
And I am very hairy,
I am very tough
And I like to play rough,
Roar, roar, that's my name,
Roar, roar, that's my game.

I live in a bin
And my favourite drink is gin,
I live in the toon
And my best friend is a baboon,
Roar, roar, that's where,
Roar, roar, don't you dare.

James McCall (11)
Elmvale Primary School

My Mum

My mum has shiny blue eyes
My mum has blonde wavy hair
I make her giggle when I tickle her
My mum sings when she's happy
I cheer her up when she's sad

My mum is so nice
My mum is joyful
My mum makes me laugh
My mum is so bright
The sun shines when my mum's happy

When my sister, brother and I get my mum cross
She sends us upstairs to think about what we have done wrong
And when we come back downstairs
We say sorry and my mum's happy again.

Kirsti Wallace (10)
Elmvale Primary School

My Special Place In Space

Way out far,
Beyond the stars,
There is a place,
I call Mars.

It's big and red,
As I said,
With aliens lying in their beds.

Their beady eyes and great big heads,
Gives me nightmares in my bed,
I sometimes shout, I sometimes scream
And I sometimes feel like a jelly bean.

Amy Buchanan (11)
Elmvale Primary School

I'm A Celebrity Get Me Out Of Here!

10 went into the jungle
Only 3 remain, Kerry, Jennie and Peter too,
Which one will it be?
We'll just have to wait and see!
I hour to go, everyone getting ready for their
Bushtukka challenges,
Kerry first, no luck,
Peter next, successful and Jennie last,
Fish eyeballs, no problemo.
The results are coming in
And Ant and Dec are just about to see who
Is the winner of 'I'm a Celebrity Get Me Out Of Here!
3 . . . 2 . . . 1 . . . it's Kerry!

Jamie Walker (11)
Elmvale Primary School

Space Race

I think? Vroom vroom went the cars
At the starting line
Zooming through Jupiter and Saturn
The cars stopped at the lights
Here comes Keiron with his car going
Chuck-a-chuck-chuck
They're just about finished
Now they take a break and have a KitKat
But Keiron is coming
Here he is and wins the race.

Brady Graham (11)
Elmvale Primary School

Scream Saturday

The midnight night is closing in,
The moon is shining like the sun,
The owls hooting looking for food,
Footsteps tapping coming to get you.

Wolves are howling at the moon,
Blood is dripping everywhere you look,
You see shadows creeping by,
Walking past the graveyard waiting for a surprise.

The haunted house is glowing yellow,
Ghosts getting ready to haunt
And the footsteps of the monsters coming closer,
Do not go out on a full moon Saturday.

The foolish boy creaks open the door,
Not knowing what's in store,
The monsters smell him,
Getting ready for their supper.

The boy's friends can't believe he's done it,
They think he's brave,
But he's just as scared,
The only thing is that he doesn't know,
He's walked to his grave.

Stacey Graham (11)
Elmvale Primary School

The Mystery Wind

The mystery wind flies through the air,
Picks up people, things, anything it can,
Three times stronger every time,
The mystery wind flies,
People fly, cars jump,
The mystery wind, bye-bye.

Thomas Graham (11)
Elmvale Primary School

The Moonlight Howl

One howl on a creepy and sleepy moonlit night,
Seven owls dancing and screeching,
Eleven grouping dancing loopy ghosts,
One thousand screaming children.

Windows flapping and creaking,
Lightning rowling and growling
Wind blowing fast and furious

Bodies clamp against sharp and lonely stones
Blood all over the place

Creepy crawlies hunting for flesh
Bats flittering past.

Leanne Little (12)
Elmvale Primary School

Summer Breeze

The summer breeze is in the trees, swaying in the air,
With bumblebees eating any honey that is spare
And the little white bunny chasing flies with no care,
The butterflies flutter by dancing in the light summer air.

Rachael Carey (11)
Elmvale Primary School

Spring

I open the window
And look out to
The garden on the first
Spring day,
I hear the bees buzzing
Round the flowers,
The thrush in the tree
And the humming bird.
I hear the sweet music,
I see the squirrel running up the tree,
The baby lambs hopping
In the green grass.

Abigail Martin (8)
Howgate Primary School

Summer

Summer, we love it!
But thunderstorms!
In paddling pools you get wet,
But lots of ice cream you get.
There's lots of lovely sun
And you get baked like a hot cross bun.
In summer you run,
It is really fun!
There are buttercups
And pansies on lots of land,
In the summer, warm and bright.

Jenny Johnston (8)
Howgate Primary School

Winter Is Beautiful

Winter is fun.
Winter is freezing.
Winter is happy.

Winter is the one.
Winter is white.
Winter is all about snow.
Winter is frosty.
People make snowmen!
People have snowball fights.
People sledging, people snowboarding.
Fingers very numb!
It is exciting in winter.
There are icicles on the window ledge.
Winter is chilly.

Martin Swapp (10)
Howgate Primary School

Winter

Winter is beautiful
And white,
When the snow falls
All through the night.
Then when I see snow
I jump up and down,
I see the icicles hanging
From my window.
I turn on my light,
My eyes light up with delight!

Marie McGeachie (9)
Howgate Primary School

Autumn

In autumn the leaves fall down
In a whirl of red, gold and brown
Outside in the garden
In the crisp white frost
I feel warm in my jumper
As I pick up acorns
Ripe apples falling and dropping
Leaves covering the garden
Like a blanket
In my bed I am almost cold
I can't sleep, the wind is blowing
When I wake up, I rush outside
I slip and fall on the grass
The wind blows and I feel leaves
On my face
They are crimson and orange
I jump up trying to pick crab apples
I see a chestnut tree
A chestnut falls on my head
It was dropped by a squirrel.

Caitlin Reid (9)
Howgate Primary School

Summer

Summer is exciting
Wearing all my T-shirts and shorts
My favourite time of year!
I feel all the fresh air
I love how the sun shines
I love eating limes
As well!

Olivia Bird (8)
Howgate Primary School

Autumn

Today's the day
With the leaves
On the way
Down past our knees
Red, brown, orange, yellow
Followed by rusty golden and bees
Look at the leaves looking at me
I feel free
If my friends were playing tig
They wouldn't catch me!
Then I see a little squirrel
Eating nuts and a little squeal!
I think he saw a fox
Bouncing up and then
He drops!
When I come near, he's off
With a flash of his crimson tail
Then the nuts, chestnuts, loads more
Not forgetting the acorn
That fell at morn
As the leaves are falling they are
Whirling and swirling
They fall to the ground
Fir cones rolling in the wind
There's something to be found
And I think it's what's hard to find
It's a box
I open it and out flies . . .
Leaves.

Amy Steel (8)
Howgate Primary School

A Robot

As the thoughtful mechanic works all day and night,
In his old shed the clink and clank goes on,
As he walks through all the nuts and bolts,
He sees it and says, 'I have made a robot!'
Then he thinks of a name for the robot,
His clever brain says to itself *clank*,
'What a jolly good name for a robot.'
He takes the robot for a test run,
It turns and says, 'My bolt's loose,' in his most scientific voice.
The mechanic fixes the loose bolt on his leg,
The robot asks him his name,
He says his name is Ratchet,
Then without a peep he walks forward,
Suddenly there is big crash,
The wrench slipped out of his hand,
What a strange dream.

Douglas McLean (9)
Humbie Primary School

Jessica

Want to know something about me . . .

   J is for jolly
   E is for elegant
   S is for smiley
   S is for sarcastic
   I is for incredible
   C is for creative
   A is for active

Yes! And that's me.

Jessica Cotterill (10)
Hutton Primary School

My Friends

Jessica likes blue
and loves Winnie the Pooh!

Isobel likes blue too
do you?

Gwen likes pink
I think!

Kate likes purple
But I've never seen a purple turtle!

Rachel likes red
a bit like her bed!

I like green, purple, blue and black.

So that just sums up all my colourful friends
and that's the end of that.

Emma Singleton (11)
Hutton Primary School

My Spell

One little frog's leg,
Two big snakes' eggs,
One cat eye
And a dead fly
To make this guy cry!

Conor O'Neill (10)
Hutton Primary School

Poems

Sorry no poems today
Maybe March or maybe May
But no poems today
I'm very sorry to say!

Gwen Dupre (10)
Hutton Primary School

Max And Billy

I've got a dog called Max
He likes to relax
He is very funny
But he doesn't want to eat honey
That's my dog called Max

I've got a dog called Billy
He is very silly
He likes to run and jump
And then he lies down with a thump
That's my dog called Billy.

Kate Jackson (10)
Hutton Primary School

Sawing

Saw and saw
And saw and saw
Back and forward
Cutting wood for shelves
And doors
A joiner's friend
For walls and floors.

Craig Scott (10)
Hutton Primary School

1, 2, 3, 4, Pick It Up

1, 2, 3, 4, 1, 2, 3, 4,   pick up some litter
                          pick up some litter

1, 2, 3, 4, 1, 2, 3, 4,   pick up some trash
                          pick up some trash

1, 2, 3, 3, 1, 2, 3, 4,   put it in the trash bin
                          trash bin, trash bin

1, 2, 3, 4, 1, 2, 3, 4,   don't be a litterbug!
                          Don't be a littlebug!

Adam Cotterill (9)
Hutton Primary School

Valentines

I love you so much,
But I can never, never tell,
Even though you sometimes
Scream and shout and yell.

The first time I saw you,
I knew that you'd be mine.
I will always love you,
If you kiss me all the time.

I'll bring you red, red roses
And chocolates you can eat
And I'll give you heart-shaped cards
That say you are so sweet.

I'll buy all the things you want,
I'll make up a lovely rhyme,
Oh! I hope that you will be
My loving Valentine.

Taylor McIntyre & Stephanie Auld (10)
Kinneil Primary School

Valentine

Love is like a candle, burning in the night
and love is like a slow dance beneath the pale moonlight.
Love is like the stars way up shining bright
and love is like a kiss and then you hold me tight.

Robyn Burns (9)
Kinneil Primary School

The Knight And The Dragon

'Let the battle commence,' said the referee,
Look out here comes the dragon and he's got a huge bee.
'Argh!' said the knight as he got a fright,
Get out the way or he might bite.
The knight got out his sword as he hoped for the award,
The knight was getting bored so he stabbed the dragon and the bee.
So the referee said the trusty, rusty knight was the winner.

Sean Cruikshank (10)
Kirkpatrick Fleming Primary School

Sheep

S heep are great, they're good for a pet
H ay is to feed the sheep in the cold winter
E xcited I am when I see the nice small lambs
E xercise is good for sheep, they jump in the air and dance about
P ortable trailers for the sheep to carry them here and there.

Thomas Illingworth (10)
Kirkpatrick Fleming Primary School

Nat, The Cat

I have a cat
Her name is Nat
She is not very fat
Most of the day
She just lays and lays
And doesn't have a care in the world
But at night she gives everyone a fright
She comes in at 12
With a mouse in her mouth
In the morning she wakes with a yawn
And purrs round my legs
I give her some milk and tuna fish
After breakfast she goes and plays
With her toys and all the boys.

Phoebe Lockhart (10)
Kirkpatrick Fleming Primary School

Rain, It's A Pain

I hate the rain, it's a pain
When it starts to drop, I want it to stop,
When out comes the sun, I feel free to run
And when it snows, I want to go out,
So why don't I like rain? Because it's a pain,
When it's pouring, it is so boring,
It drops, it drops, *splash!*

Conor Smith (10)
Kirkpatrick Fleming Primary School

Fay's Day

I have a cat
She is so very fat
Her name is Fay
And she eats all day

In her basket she sleeps
On the floor, by the door
Dreaming peacefully of bats
And then of tasty rats

She wakes and tiptoes to the kitchen
She looks at me with her bright green eyes
You can see she is longing for pies
She heads to her dish

Expecting her favourite fish
But instead she finds a cod
She thinks it looks very odd
She has never seen a cod
But she wolfs it down all the same
Then goes to play a game.

Danielle Story (11)
Kirkpatrick Fleming Primary School

Kittens!

Kittens are careful
They're very playful
They like to sleep
And dream lovely dreams
If you awake her, you're very daring
So there's a lesson about kittens
Do not annoy them when they're chewing mittens.

Kirsty Prentice (9)
Kirkpatrick Fleming Primary School

Rosie

I have a dog called Rosie
She is a little bit nosey

Rosie is a Westie
She is a bit of a pestie

Rosie thinks she is a Labrador
Because I have two more Labradors

Rosie is playful
Rosie is grateful

Rosie is never white
And it is never a fright to see her not white

When she comes home with a bone.

Isabella Graham-Campbell (9)
Kirkpatrick Fleming Primary School

Crazy Animals

Animals can come in all different shapes and sizes
My bat thinks he's a cat
It eats and peeps and creeps
My bat chases my rat

My rat had a cat
My cat ate my rat
My cat chases my hog
Up, down, round and round

My hog thinks it's a frog
It jumps up and down and round in the pond
It chases the flies in and out
The hog almost killed my frog.

Kirsty Hotchkiss (10)
Kirkpatrick Fleming Primary School

The World Cup

T he match that everyone had been waiting for
H ere it is the World Cup
E arly at half-past twelve it is about to start
W ait for it and kick-off
O ff they go
R eally a fantastic game so far
L ater on a goal!
'D on't cry,' said a player to their goalie
C lose game but Brazil had defeated Germany
U p the cup went in the winner's hand
P laced in the trophy cabinet at Brazil.

Cameron Lockhart (10)
Kirkpatrick Fleming Primary School

Pigs

Pigs always sleep
In the muck; smelly
Smelly horrible muck
Pigs make grunting noises
And chase you
Because they want to
Eat you, my piggy ate
Billy, my cat.

Leanne Postlethwaite (10)
Kirkpatrick Fleming Primary School

Tractors Are Great On A Farm

T ractors are very good on a farm
R adiators are in the tractor to keep it going
A n accelerator keeps the tractor going on the road
C ase is the name of the tractor
T ractors are good at saving time on baling
O n the farm it will work like gold
R adiators are also to keep the tractor warm and cool
S oft tracks make the tractors bounce.

Conor Allan (9)
Kirkpatrick Fleming Primary School

The Celts And Romans

Fierce and ferocious the Romans fought,
Well organised and wild,
Made the Celts so cross,
Dark, deadly road digging Romans,
Defeated Boudica's tired tribe.
Bad Romans burned Boudica's chariots,
Leaving them lying, lost to die.

Bryar Mennie (8)
Knowepark Primary School

Flower, Oh Flowers

F lower, oh flowers.
L ove is in the air.
O h how you smell.
W onder of you is in the world.
E veryone through their nose.
R unning through their nose.
S isters and mums love you.
   How the smell of your beauty gets into our lives.

Cameron Younger (8)
Knowepark Primary School

A Big Battle

Long, long ago,
Two armies met
Boudica's and Claudius'
The battle commenced!

The dreadful deadly Romans
Attacked ferocious and fast,
Killing the feeble Celts,
Dry dust and dirt flying everywhere.

The hairy Celt warriors
Were beaten on that day,
The Romans in their heavy armour,
Survived and marched away.

Kieran Challinor (8)
Knowepark Primary School

Ponies

Ponies, ponies are so nice,
Galloping around all night,
Ponies are so nice,
They like to race,
Long ones, short ones.

In the field at night,
They gently close their eyes,
Lying down on a bed of grass,
Till the sun rises.

Sarah McColm (8)
Knowepark Primary School

Romans

Dangerous, deadly Romans march,
Defeating the Celts at Danum.
Celts crying into battle,
Came crashing to the ground.

Tired Romans terrify the Britons,
Their armour as heavy as rocks,
Driving Celts away from round houses,
Knocking them to the ground.

The Romans came into battle,
Then set up their camp for the night,
Digging a ditch around their camp,
To place some wooden stakes.

They march onto another place
And kills most of the local people,
Building more buildings for them to stay,
A Roman army on campaign.

They then defeat the Celtic country
And batter Boudica's children.
So Boudica drinks some poison,
To leave this life for death.

Andrew Anderson (8)
Knowepark Primary School

Roman Alliteration

Careful Claudius attacked the coast,
Tired teams of Romans camped
Their tents of eight as warm as toast
Did hard work every day
But sailed back to Gaul to stay.

Tiffany Duncan (8)
Knowepark Primary School

Beginning Of Time

Long, long ago, there was a big bang
That is when time first began.
The universe formed from rocks and dust,
The other planets formed from the ones that had bust!

Life had begun from the heat of the sun,
So every planet had now spun,
You use a telescope at night to look at the stars
And the very red planet you see will be Mars!

So Earth has a moon, that men have explored,
Leaving the moon then the rocket ship roared,
Now everyone knows the history of space,
Then the rocket ship landed back into place.

Jack Borthwick (8)
Knowepark Primary School

Romans

Claudius cantered on horses towards the Celts,
The rugged Roman army reached Ratae - Coritanorum
Punching people and powering past the Celts,
Deadly, dangerous and dreaded Romans dying in deep ditches,
Shields saving soldiers from swords and arrows,
The king was killed and so too the kids,
Big Boudica bashing the Romans badly,
But toughly trained Romans finally beat the Celts,
Great and good Boudica drank a glass of poison,
Slipping silently to her death.

Alex Carroll (8)
Knowepark Primary School

Romans

The clever red Romans
Defeated the Celtic country
Brainy Romans attacking Britain
In the year of 54BC

The silly sly Celts
Creep towards the Roman camp
Their tribe trying to attack
The dangerous and dastardly Romans.

Liam Murray (8)
Knowepark Primary School

The Romans Attack

The tough and terrifying Romans tried
Torturing beautiful Boudica's daughters
When the Romans battered the Celts to bits
Fighting fire in open land
Where the Romans led the Celts.

Hamish Robinson (8)
Knowepark Primary School

The Roman Story

The Roman army is astounding
Bad Romans battering the Celtic houses
The battle was deadly and demanding
The result disgusting and damaging
The small sleek boats set sail
Swiftly back to Rome.

Mairi Chisholm (8)
Knowepark Primary School

The Romans

Each day the Romans were busy,
The Romans battered Boudica's children.
Many men marching mercilessly,
That day tired Romans lay.

The rugged Romans reached for riches,
The Romans as strong as oxes.
Such good fighters and so dangerous,
Battling bravely with lots of weapons.

Invading lots of places,
Their tents as warm as toast,
Building lots of clever things,
Hadrian's wall and many straight roads.

Shelley McLeish (8)
Knowepark Primary School

Invasion!

The Romans were such a lucky lot,
With swords and shields to fit a king.
Hadrian's wall, the Picts attacked,
With many ladders and fierce men.

The Celts would drive them back,
Off the land and down the hill.
Out of Scotland and into England,
Where the invaders belonged.

Andrew Nichol (8)
Knowepark Primary School

My Pony

My pony is small and cute,
She enjoys a carrot or two,
We gallop along the route,
There are four of us in a queue!

Emily Anderson (8)
Knowepark Primary School

A Spirit Star

A spirit star up in the dark sky,
A spirit star so low,
I can't believe I saw you up there,
I really hope you will never go.

You sparkle and shine up there alone,
You can sparkle and make it bright,
You're nice, you're sending spirits high,
Your blazing twinkle ever so light.

I cannot see the sun anymore,
Your light has covered every other star,
The flowers grow, but the rain's just a trickle,
I hope you'll send your spirits far.

Iona Matheson (8)
Knowepark Primary School

The Romans

A long time ago there was a king,
The deadly Romans defeated Colchester easily.
The Romans marched onto London fast,
The Celts making a mad run for the Romans.

Big bulging Boudica bashed the Romans,
Fighting them fair and square,
The Romans marched fast, but
The rugged Celts came to batter them fair,
But Boudica poured herself a pot of poison!

Alastair Penny (8)
Knowepark Primary School

A Young Brown Pony

The pony walks in the deep green grass,
She eats and eats all day.
She cannot stop, she loves it so much,
When she is in the best spot she will stay.

She doesn't mind if you pat her,
She will neigh and neigh
And will not stop,
She even likes to buck and play!

She can nip, but it will not bleed,
Her shaggy coat gets in the way.
She does not like to be left alone,
People always stop, look and stay.

Evie Anderson (8)
Knowepark Primary School

My Sister

My sister is really funny,
My sister has long hair.
She is fun, her hair shining,
Like the blazing sun.

She is an animal lover,
She is so smart and clever,
She is eleven years old
And horses are her hobby.

Craig Bruce (8)
Knowepark Primary School

My Special Unicorn

My special unicorn is so cheerful,
A pillow lying under her head,
I say she is so beautiful,
As I tuck her into bed.

She is so cool and purpley-blue,
For she's a lilac-scented unicorn
And when we go to the cinema,
She always eats my popcorn!

You smell so nice,
You have your rights
And wrongs as well,
But I doubt it!

You sparkle so bright
And let out light,
Her name is Mystical
And guess who named her? *Me!*

Caitlin Tait (8)
Knowepark Primary School

A Celtic House

A Celtic house is really old,
A Celtic house is really cold!
Full of dark smoke, dirt and stew,
A Celtic house is for the bold!

A Celtic house is really smelly,
I saw a Celt with a hairy belly!
A Celtic house is really round,
The Celtic people guard their ground.

Adam Nichol (8)
Knowepark Primary School

What Is Black?

My colour looks like
Space without the planets
And stars twinkling in it
Black is a cave without
A torch light
Black is the starry sky at
Night and the only
Light is the moon
My colour feels like
A black man's hand
My colour feels like
Space itself
Black feels beautiful
Black, black boots going
Thump, thump, thump
On the stairs
My colour smells like
Beautiful, beautiful peppermint chocolate
My colour smells like
A fire that has been put out
But there is still
Black smoke in the air
My colour sounds like
Car tyres screeching in a skid
My colour tastes like
Lovely Coca-Cola
My colour tastes like
Burnt chocolate chip cookies and burnt toast.

Matthew McEwan (10)
Letham Primary School

What Is Black?

At night I feel sleepy
Watching the pitch-black air
Blowing on me
A car is racing to work
An evil Goth
An animal trying to catch its prey
Someone is listening to a blaring telly
Silence is around me
But what about space?
I am riding my new black skateboard
At the seaside!

Brian Dibben (10)
Letham Primary School

What Is Blue?

The sky is blue
Like a blueberry
Blue feels like water
The wind and the waves
And the drip drop of rain
It feels stretchy like Blu-tack
It tastes like bubblegum juice
And chewing gum.

Douglas McAdam (8)
Letham Primary School

What Is Red?

Red is evil eyes, the Devil's face
The demons, the red snake
The red skull, red is lava
Red is the underworld
Red is vampire teeth
Red is raw meat and Mars
Red is hot spiky and jaggy
Red is fire
Red is loud screams dripping blood
Red is strawberry, red is spicy
And hot chilli.

Shaun Wilson (10)
Letham Primary School

Emotions

Heart racer
Stomach churner
Breath taker
Soul shaker
Throat choker
Nail biter
Lip locker
Brain banger
Body booster.

Jamie Rae (11)
Locharbriggs Primary School

Promises

Promises are always bringing hope and joy,
    they make people happy when skies are grey.

There are promises we keep
    and promises we break.

When you keep a promise
    you feel happy and successful.

When you break a promise
    you feel guilty and down in the dumps.

Promises are all around us,
    big ones, small ones, all day long.

When you keep a promise,
    you make someone happy.

When you break a promise,
    you let someone down.

You feel great when you make someone happy,
    but you feel silly when you let someone down.

So take my word
    and rely on promises!

Hannah Irving (11)
Locharbriggs Primary School

A Walk In The Woods

Soft like a bag of feathers,
The branch sharp like thorns.
The wind whistling through the leaves,
Rough like sandpaper.
Walking slow like a ghost in a graveyard.
Crunching on the ground like stone.
They bark as a gun lets off.
Birds singing to each other.
The long walk feels like a day gone by
And at last the walk is over and the sun shines as bright as ever.

Stacey Cullen (11)
Locharbriggs Primary School

Dracula The Devil

Dracula the devil, most gruesome in the world
Hair pitch-black like a witch's cauldron
Ready to attack
Eyes are red like a burning fire
Tatty old black coat rough as can be
And black pointed horns like blood-sharp fangs
Awakes ratty from his deep sleep
His dusty medieval coffin
He climbs out steadily from his coffin
To the big open world
Creeps sluggishly through the dark streets
Like a poisonous frog
Slides under the door
Like a slimy snake
Twists your neck like an old barn owl
Too late to run
Too late to hide
You'll be next!

Amie Byers (11)
Locharbriggs Primary School

I Was . . .

I was Sally Rainbow
I was cool
I was colourful
I wore loads of make-up and had this ultra-hip hairstyle
I wore the most amazing sexy clothes
I had pierced ears and a stud in my nose
I didn't have a mum
I didn't have a dad
I lived all by myself in this incredible flat
Sometimes my friends stayed over at my place
I had heaps of friends and they all begged me to be their best friend!

Eilidh McRobert (11)
Locharbriggs Primary School

Bob

There was a man called Bob
Who had a big gob
He did too much talking
And not enough walking

Bob was a very fat man
He couldn't fit in a van
He had a small house
And a little pet mouse

His house was full of food
And he was very rude
One day he got run over
And was buried in Dover

That was the end of Bob
Who had a big gob.

Scott Padmore (11)
Locharbriggs Primary School

Sun

The sun is very sunny
The sun is like a treat
I love to play and dance all day
When the sun is in my street.

Ryan Learmont (11)
Locharbriggs Primary School

Why?
(Dedicated to Mya Rose Davidson)

Why is the sky blue?
Why is the grass green?
Why is a summer day
Such a beautiful scene?

Why does a feather float?
Why is there such expectation
On the voyage of a boat?

Why do I wonder why?
Why do I have friends that wander by?
Why do so many people have to die
In this great wide world?
All you can do is wonder
Why?

John Darren Davidson (11)
Locharbriggs Primary School

Friends

Friends are great,
Friends are fun,
Friends are the best,
All year round,
If you want to have fun,
Get friends
And have fun.

Jade Aitken (11)
Locharbriggs Primary School

Why?

A tear flows down your face
I am in grimace
Every day I pray
That you will stay
Every night I cry
For I know one day you will die
Why do you block up all this stress?
You know as well as I do, it'll end up in a mess
Lie down - have a rest
For I will treat you like a guest
Let it all at ease
Please!
I hate to see you like this
I'll give you a hug and a kiss
Cheer you up
Have tea in a cup
Your eye fills up with water
Why do you cry?
Why are you sad?
I don't understand
I'm in a twist
It's like a foggy mist

We're back at the start
I can finally feel how it is to have a kindred heart
I'm older now
We've had a row
I know how it feels
But your heart heals.

Marita Barr (11)
Locharbriggs Primary School

The Art Of The Vampire

Night's creature
Bad feature
Night's creature
Never a preacher

As black as a shadow
Behind your back
As cold as a heart
That couldn't bear to part

Night's creature
Calling my name

Craving the blood
Mine, maybe

Night's creature
Clawing at my back

Craving the dark
It's all over by the break of day

Sleep until the next 200 years
Then the blood will be repaid.

Sophie Russell (11)
Loretto Junior School

Tell Me!

Tell me why
Why did you do it?
For me or for you?
The money or the greed?
The pleasure or the pity?

Edward Dudgeon (10)
Loretto Junior School

Scotland

A bonnie land o' burns an' braes
With glens and gulleys narrow
A feast of a sight, for a nation so small
With a history pushing it on

Warbling birds roaming free
O'er the banks o' the Doon an' Firth
Lads and lassies playin' on
Till they themselves pass on

Then 'ere was a queen o' Scots
Whose power and glory faded
But even Edward cowered before her
With 'is armies great an' powerful
We 'ave risen now an' again
But this time is for true!

Harry Marriott & Alexander Byers (10)
Loretto Junior School

Kennings

It's a good scab picker,
It's a memory holder,
You write with it,
You draw pictures with it,
You use it to put on nail varnish,
It's a great shaker
And a weight taker,
You eat with it
And use it a lot,
A lifesaver

What am I?

Danielle Walton (10)
Loretto Junior School

Penny

Penny was a bonnie lassie,
Wearing a wee blue dress,
Her father was a funny man,
Who didnae really rest.

One morn wee Penny said, 'I won't!'
Her father didnae grin,
She wouldnae go and work that day
And pricked him with a pin.

'Och! Ye wee lass!' her father said,
'I willnae greet, noo go tae bed!'
But no! The lass ran awaw,
She didnae come back that day, ataw.

Her mother was greetin', 'It's all ye fault,
You shouldnae have let her go!'
Their son called Sam said, 'I'll go oot!'
And trailed through the cold, freezin' snow.

Noo they're both oot, the wee young bairns,
Oot wi' the wee chirpin' birds.
Oot alone, nae company,
A' alone, a' alone, a' alone . . .

Then Granny came haeme,
Wi' snow on her boots.
Then came the bairns haeme too,
'I found them outside playin' aboot,
Hittin' me poor black ol' shoe.'

'I,' said Granny, 'say it was them,
Playing' aboot wi' the snow.'
Sam said, 'No!' Granny said, 'Yes!'
'An' it's all cos of Penny in the wee blue dress!'

Megan Selley (10)
Loretto Junior School

Dolphin

The dolphin is a bluey-grey colour
It is like the aqua-blue sea

It has a long bottled nose with an extremely long body
Its fin is like a blunt thorn

A dolphin's eye is about the same size as our eyes
It is as smooth as new glass

The dolphin swims like someone doing running stitch
It goes into the water like a bomb

The dolphin sleeps under the water in caves
But it comes up every so often because it needs to breathe
or it will die!

It is a very good communicator
It is as smart as a 12-year-old boy or girl

A group of dolphins is called a school of dolphins
A dolphin eats fish, it dives down to catch its prey

The school of dolphins jumps in and out of the water very fast
The dolphins jump out of the water and they dive down to
catch their prey

When the dolphin is in the water
It swims through the lovely smooth turquoise sea.

Rebecca Scott (11)
Murrayburn Primary School

Dolphin

The dolphin is as smooth as a glass bottle lying on the beach,
Gliding through the sea looking for its prey,
Moving through the ocean like a graceful dancer,
As blue as the clear sky on a sunny day,
Swimming under the water only its fin is out,
It is more intelligent than a five year old boy just starting school,
Diving low and jumping high, that's where the waves will take it.

Scott McDonald (11)
Murrayburn Primary School

Otter

The otter skin is brown and furry,
It eats its fish up in a hurry,
It likes to play with all its friends,
Until the long day ends.

Its feet are webbed and move quite quickly,
Its skin is smooth and soft and silky.
An otter's eyes are shiny and brown,
When it sees a fish it dives right down.

An otter's shape is long and thin,
It is sometimes hunted for its skin.
An otter swims about in its troop,
A troop is the name of its family group.

Otters live in the deep blue sea,
My favourite animal it may be.
An otter is very smart,
It swims through the water like a speeding dart.

An otter's favourite game is tig,
Its skin is like a smooth flat wig.
When the day is over and it falls asleep,
You won't hear out of it a peep.

Martin Hickey (11)
Murrayburn Primary School

Dolphin

Dolphin, as smooth as a sheet of glass,
Skin as grey as the stormy sky,
It moves like a streak of lighting,
The amazing sound ripples through the sea,
It dives like a bomb from the sky heading straight for the sea,
It jumps out and lands like a volcano of water ready to erupt,
Chasing like a policeman catching his prey,
All day long it bolts in the water looking for fish and playing,
As smart as a 5 year old boy ready for school,
They travel in a school of children bursting to get out to play,
In school they face the shark but on their own they hide,
They are special; one of a kind,
While they play they sing like a choir of angels from Heaven,
Very friendly and ready for action to defeat enemies.

Kimberley Dunn (11)
Murrayburn Primary School

My Blue Dolphin

My dolphin is as blue as a sapphire,
It is as smooth as the pebbles on the sand,
She laughs and plays,
She is as smart as a child,
As graceful as a ballerina as she dives and soars through the sea,
Her tail and her fins are her engine and steering wheels,
Her nose is a bottle as smooth as glass,
Her skin is a radar, it helps her to hear,
My dolphin eats fish, how much I don't know,
But when a shark comes by, she hides,
Then she is safe,
When she swims with her school,
I can always tell which one she is,
Because my dolphin is one of a kind.

Nicola Robertson (11)
Murrayburn Primary School

A Poem About Dolphins

A dolphin is as smooth as a whipped ice cream
A dolphin is like blue and grey with silver shining through it
A dolphin is sleek and kind to man and woman
A dolphin is like a bird gliding through the sky
With a glimmer of light
It lives in the ice-cold waters of the sea
It eats slimy fish
It catches these by soaring through the water
Like a fast drill wanting to crack something open!
It feels like cold shiny buttons in a tub
Its eyes are like sapphires sitting in a cold bucket
Flippers as graceful as a butterfly fluttering in the sky . . .

Sara Willis (11)
Murrayburn Primary School

A Dolphin Poem

As grey as a misty, winter morning
As smooth as a piece of velvet cloth,
It's like a human diving into the sea
It's like a radar speaking to its friends
It's a darting arrow going through the sea
A school of dolphins diving in and out of the sea looking for prey
Jumping up to the sky and diving into the sea
Looking for gleaming fish
Here's a school of playful dolphins ready to play
As clever as a five-year-old schoolchild
Looking to learn new things . . .

Sara Bavidge (11)
Murrayburn Primary School

The Battle Of Stirling Bridge

The English soldiers battled it out with the Scottish,
Scottish soldiers trooped around the English soldiers,
Soldiers died *wham* while other soldiers died *bam*,
Bam, a soldier dropped with a *thud*,
Thud! Blood gushed out of the soldier's head,
Heads fell on the ground as the battle went on,
On and on the battle went as people were risking their lives,
Lives were taken without the English even getting touched, *splatter*,
Splatter went the marsh as the English soldiers had them cornered,
Cornered they were, *swoosh* went an arrow gliding like a
                                                bird to its prey,
The prey were the English while the bird was the Scottish,
Scottish soldiers swarmed the area and surrounded the English,
English soldiers were very worried and scared,
Scared they were that they surrendered,
Surrendered they did and they got captured by the Scottish,
Scottish soldiers were celebrating as William Wallace declared victory,
Victory was theirs for the taking.

Corey Robertson (11)
Murrayburn Primary School

The Battle Of Stirling Bridge

Heavy armour on the weary bodies of the English on the
                                       way to Stirling Castle,
Castle of Stirling is overtaken by the English,
English soldiers unaware of the Scots clanking along the Scots came,
Thundering down the path and destroyed the English,
English got clattered, the bridge was destroyed
And the English went flying into the river like a meteor hitting Earth.
Earth had an echo of noise
Of clashing swords, axes, arrows and shields,
The marsh holding the English down,
Letting the arrows melt through the armour of the English,
English were defeated and victory went to William Wallace.

Ryan Lee (10)
Murrayburn Primary School

The Battle Of Stirling Bridge

The soldiers march fearlessly to Stirling Bridge,
Stirling Bridge was not far away
And you could hear the soldiers' armour clattering together.
Together the soldiers went over Stirling Bridge
Like magnets attracted to Stirling Castle,
Stirling Castle was safe behind the Scottish army,
The Scottish army attacked the English
And they began the battle of Stirling Bridge
Like a shark chasing its prey for dinner.
Dinner was what everybody wanted
And also they wanted to win the battle.
Battle was happening and they were falling over the bridge
Into the marsh, squishing and squashing
Everywhere thrown out into the water,
Water was splashing everywhere like a big gush of
                              wind blowing everywhere,
Everywhere was arrows slicing the air and hitting the soldiers,
Soldiers were fighting back and you could hear the swords
And shields clashing together like the water and the sand.
Sand was nowhere to be seen because the soldiers were sinking
Slowly to their death into the sand.
Sand was not where William Wallace was
Because he was still fighting against the English.
English were slowly but surely giving up,
Giving up was not what the Scots were doing,
Because they were going to win as there was only about twenty left.
Twenty left of the English army so they began to back away
Like babies not wanting their dolls house because they
                              knew they'd lost.
Lost the English did and the Scots won *The Battle of Stirling Bridge.*

Katie Flockhart (11)
Murrayburn Primary School

The Battle of Stirling Bridge

English soldiers marching towards Stirling Castle,
Castle was cold and very dark and made of stone
Stones are used for weapons and bows and arrows and swords
Swords scraping, chinging, screams as a soldier dies in battle
Battling people falling in the marsh
Marsh, splash, plop, squidge, slip
Slipping into the water
Water sploshing like a thousand diamonds
As the horses and soldiers are falling in
The Scottish soldier moved in to get victory
And win more of the castle back
Backing away from the castle
Scotland are winning more victories
A toast for winning more victories
Cheers tomorrow as we win more castles
Castle English have taken Stirling Castle
They want war, we will give them war
We will get them from behind
They won't expect it
William Wallace had a trick up that little sleeve of his.

Dale Brown (11)
Murrayburn Primary School

The Battle Of Stirling Bridge

The Scottish marched heavily into battle as loud as thunder!
Sneaking past the English on horseback
Hooves thudding on the ground
Clanging swords as they run into battle
Horses' hooves smacking on the ground
Ground covered by the English ready to kill
Blood splatting on the ground
On the ground the sound of chains getting struck
King Edward's raging!
As many arrows come shooting out of trees
Striking the English
As the English started to retreat
They only had eight men left on the field
What a great glory for the Scots
And Wallace!

Brian Dudgeon (11)
Murrayburn Primary School

The Battle Of Stirling Bridge

Weary English soldiers have Stirling Castle
Castle doors would come down like a cannonball from the sky
Skies go grey when Wallace moves out with his Scots
Scots are ready to beat the English with a clash
Clash of swords battering each other
Other soldiers fall into the marsh
Marsh sucks the soldiers into the ground
Ground starts to crack as more and more soldiers head for the bridge
Bridge is almost clear of English soldiers
Soldiers of Wallace's have destroyed the English
English have failed to keep the castle
The castle is still in the hands of the Scots now!

Jamie Proudfoot (11)
Murrayburn Primary School

Dolphin

It is as blue as the dark night sky
With its eyes twinkling like the stars,
Jumping up and down like a needle
On a sewing machine; it dives into the water.
It has a white stomach that is as white as fresh snow.
Its smooth sparkling skin and flippers
Feel like sand running through your fingers,
Racing through the cold waters catching fish on the way,
Living in the sea, dolphins are always on the move with their school,
Its call is like an old party hooter,
When it's in danger it will hide for its life,
It's as smart as a five-year-old child starting school for the first time!

Jean Welsh (11)
Murrayburn Primary School

The Battle Of Stirling Bridge

The Scottish soldiers standing through the countryside
Countryside as bare as a blank page blowing in the breeze
Breeze was extremely heavy as a knight's armour
Armour sparks when arrows clash against it
It was a remarkable battle with the English and Scottish
Scottish jumped the English soldiers on Stirling Bridge
William Wallace and many more Scottish soldiers
Soldiers of Scotland declared victory over England.

Christopher Robertson (11)
Murrayburn Primary School

Bottlenose Dolphin

Bottlenose dolphin curved like a banana,
Blue smooth skin like glass,
Crashing and diving into the crystal blue sea,
Its long bottlenose like a cold blue ice pop
Helping it to dive into the ocean,
Fins like quarter of the moon gliding through the water,
Fish get sucked in like a hairdryer
By the amazing teeth of a dolphin,
Jumping high, diving deep it catches its prey,
As intelligent as a person, as smart as a five-year-old child,
Playful and fun dancing and showing off
To get attention like a magician performing,
Sending messages to its friends with an echo rippling through the sea.

Vikki Baigrie (11)
Murrayburn Primary School

Seal Poem

The beautiful grey seal
Its skin mottled with spots of coffee and paint
It cuts through the water racing to find its hungry prey.
Its whiskers as sharp as needles
And bottle-top eyes
Plodding on land as slow as a huge snail
But in water they're as fast as a Concorde
Swerving and turning
Sleeping in the open on rocks so cold and bare
Nothing to hear in the distance
Basking on the rocks as it waits for sunrise
Flapping its flippers.

Amanda Cameron (11)
Murrayburn Primary School

You!

You!
You are my favourite dog.
You!
You have black fur.
You!
You are funny and playful.
You!
You have floppy ears.
You!
You have green eyes.

You!
You do tricks.
You!
You are younger than me.
You!
You are funny.
You!
You are naughty sometimes.
You!
You play ball.
You!
You are called Tixey.

Josh Marshall (8)
Newington Primary School

I Feel

I feel mad when I am sad.
I feel sad when I am bad.
I feel crazy when I am nasty.
I feel happy when I am funny.
I feel nervous when I am jealous.
I feel glad when I am not bad.

Ryan Ferguson (8)
Newington Primary School

You!

You!
You always ask for money.
You!
You are a pain.
You!
You always jump on me.
You!
Your hair is a mess.
You!
You belt me.

You!
You don't share crisps.
You!
You are a good joke teller.
You!
You are older than me.
You!
You have brown hair with blonde streaks.
You!
You are skinny.
You!
You are my big sister called Kirsty.

Robbie McWhirter (7)
Newington Primary School

I Feel

I feel happy when you cuddle me.
I feel hungry when it is teatime.
I feel excited when it is my birthday.
I feel crazy when it is playtime.
I feel glad when I'm not bad.
I feel nervous when I am on my karaoke.

Zoe Harkness (8)
Newington Primary School

You!

You!
You have short brown hair.
You!
You sometimes annoy me.
You!
You have blue eyes.
You!
Your room is a mess.
You!
You never eat your tea.

You!
You are unlike any of the others.
You!
You always nip, kick, bite, punch and hit me.
You!
You always drive me up the wall.
You!
You are a good joke teller.
You!
You are cute.
You!
You are my sister called Erin.

Eilidh Wright (8)
Newington Primary School

You!

You!
You are my fuzz ball.
You!
You are always there to cheer me up.
You!
You always make the living room stink.
You!
You always lick me and make me laugh.
You!
You are black, brown and white.

You!
You are fun to play with.
You!
You, when I walk past with food you start to squeak.
You!
You are a mental guinea pig.
You!
You are a pain sometimes.
You!
You are always there for me.
You!
You are our guinea pig and we love you, Patch.

Laura Allison (8)
Newington Primary School

You!

You!
You are the best.
You!
You are my friend.
You!
You are funny.
You!
You are fast.
You!
You are nice and white.

You!
You are fast.
You!
You are heavenly.
You!
You are big.
You!
You are cool.
You!
You are sometimes bad.
You!
You are my horse, Smurf.

Logan Creighton (8)
Newington Primary School

You!

You!
You make me happy.
You!
You make me angry.
You!
You push me.
You!
You pull my hair.
You!
You make me sad.

You!
You always play.
You!
You always drive me up the wall.
You!
Your hands are dirty.
You!
You're a little pest.

Callum Rogerson (8)
Newington Primary School

You!

You!
You pull my hair.
You!
You're always a pain.
You!
You are very, very greedy.
You!
You ask for my money.
You!
You make a mess of my bed.

You!
You always have blonde hair.
You!
You have a nice smile.
You!
You have very nice clothes.
You!
You are my cousin called Ashton.

Shannon Morrin (8)
Newington Primary School

Space

Sun, moon and Milky Way,
Rockets arrive at a docking bay.

Nine planets orbit the sun,
If aliens live, I'm sure they have fun.

At night you can see lots of stars,
All of them a lot bigger than Mars.

Gavin Hogg (10)
Oxgangs Primary School

It . . .

It was scary,
It was ugly,
It was cheeky,
Stinky,
Smelly,
Thick and smiley,
It was my sister!

It was freaky,
It was tall,
It was big,
It was ugly,
It was large,
Silly,
Funny,
It was my dad!

It was nice,
It was lovely,
It was kind,
Helpful,
Very shouty,
Fine,
It was my mum!

It was an angel,
It was kind and helpful,
It was smart,
Cheeky,
Beautiful,
It was me!

Nicole Anderson (10)
Oxgangs Primary School

Books

Thick books, thin books
All different sizes
Good books, boring books
And lots, lots more

Some books cost more than others
Some cost less
Children's books are sometimes good
And adults' books are too

Take some time to read your book
And you will really like it
If you read lots and lots of books
You might become an author!

Karen Gibson (10)
Oxgangs Primary School

Jelly

I'm a wibbly wobbly jelly
And I can wibble and wobble like that
I can wibble like this
And I can wobble like that

I can shiver and shimmer on my plate
And sometimes I'm sticky if you like!

Melissa Collins (11)
Oxgangs Primary School

Nose

The smell of bacon sizzling
When I wake up in the morning
The smell of my mum's perfume
When I walk in the room
The smell of the flowers outside
The smell of the classroom
When I am sitting in my seat
The smell of pencils being sharpened
And the smell of pen's ink
The smell of the outside
Fresh and warm
The smell of my bedroom
The smell of my tea
Oh yummy!
The smell of my bed
Then *stop!*
*I see nothing
I am asleep.*

Karen Ewing (11)
Oxgangs Primary School

Pancakes

I love the smell of them on a weekend morning
And when I gradually walk down the stairs
To the glistening, lip-moistening, tender pleasure
Centre that is *pancakes*
And when I sink my teeth into its tender flesh
And the maple syrup oozes out of the side
That is good *pancakes!*

Fraser Robertson (11)
Oxgangs Primary School

A Dragon's Soul

Dragon high
Dragon spirit
Floating in the cotton clouds

Flaming heat
Gassy smoke
Sparkling all around

Blue horrid scaly wings
Whizzing through the frosty air
Never freezing in the harsh snow

Mating, then laying, then hatching
And it goes around again and again,
Dragon high, dragon fly.

Graham Dickson (10)
Oxgangs Primary School

Gargoyles

Gargoyles hang from castle walls
Gargoyles are made into ugly dolls
Gargoyles are made from rock and stones
Gargoyles have no bones
You can't buy gargoyles in shops or malls
And they're out of reach by getting hit by balls.

Nick Cross (10)
Oxgangs Primary School

The Kitten

I see a kitten waking
I see a kitten shaking
I see a kitten waking and shaking
On his little bed

I see a kitten straying
I see a kitten playing
I see a kitten straying and playing
On his little bed

I see a kitten eating
I see a kitten cheating
I see a kitten eating and cheating
On his little bed

I see a kitten chewing
I see a kitten spewing
I see a kitten chewing and spewing
On his little bed

I see a kitten resting
I see a kitten pestering
I see a kitten resting and pestering
On his little bed

I see a kitten pouncing
I see a kitten bouncing
I see a kitten pouncing and bouncing
On his little bed

I see a kitten weeping
I see a kitten sleeping
I see a kitten, a kitten.

Rachel Laing (9)
Oxgangs Primary School

Hands

Touching	Pulling	Rubbing	Stinging
Feeling	Pushing	Turning	Numb
Holding	Whipping	Scratching	Nipping
Writing	Sewing	Slapping	Tipping
Moving	Mushing	Painting	That's what my
Working	Building	Mopping	hands do for me
Moulding	Nipping	Matching	
Lighting	Mowing	Clapping.	

Adjana Mason (11)
Oxgangs Primary School

Pizza Slice

When my mum asks me what I want for tea
I say, 'A pizza slice.'
She says, 'OK, I'll go and get it in five minutes.'
Then she goes and comes back,
My mum shouts on me and puts it on the desk,
I love pizza slices,
They are lovely.

Vikki Brash (11)
Oxgangs Primary School

Love And Hate

Fluffy clouds and sunny skies
These things I love
Long queues and stuffy shops
These things I hate
Fresh cream cakes and sweets galore
These things I love even more
Rainy days and cheesy feet
There's a hate you can't defeat
Love and hate is a funny thing
Like cold snowy days in the middle of spring.

David Sivewright (11)
Oxgangs Primary School

Cats

Cats are cuddly, cats are cute,
Cats are the cutest things you'll meet,
Cats are snugly, cats are fluffy,
Cats are fat and sometimes thin,
My cat's always on my bed,
My cat's never on my sister's head,
His paws are sweet and cuddly,
I love my cat, one day he'll burst,
Oh how I love cats,
I could live with them forever and ever,
I love them so much,
They're playful and fun,
They leap around your legs.

Paula Campbell (7)
Oxgangs Primary School

Star

I am a star,
I am the shiniest star on Earth,
But I am a very small star,
I don't like being small
Because the other stars don't play with me,
I want to be the biggest star
Because I will have friends,
It is horrible not having friends.

Claire Anderson (7)
Oxgangs Primary School

Going To War

Going to war is so, so nasty,
I would never be a soldier when I grow up,
Up slashes the weapon,
Down falls the body,
As you can see, war is so nasty,
I shall be a poet when I grow up,
I shall write lots of poems
About anything I want,
About anything I choose.

Iain Mackay (7)
Oxgangs Primary School

My Life As A TV

I'm black, I'm a cuboid,
With a square glass face
And buttons all over me,
I sit on my owner's chest of drawers,
Getting bored,
But when I am used I am happy again,
My owner's favourite channels are 1 and 2,
But when the video player goes on I get jealous.

Rebecca Cork (7)
Oxgangs Primary School

The Magic Of Flowers

Flowers are so magical,
They pop up in spring,
Flowers are so colourful,
Flowers dance in the wind,
Then one day they will die away,
Then they will come back another day.

Rachael Erskine (7)
Oxgangs Primary School

My Budgie

My budgie is big,
My budgie bites,
He is round,
He can be found,
He does not come out of his cage,
He eats birdseed,
My budgie drinks water,
In the daytime he doesn't play with his toys,
My budgie plays with his toys at night,
My budgie sits on his perch,
He jumps on his cage when the wind blows.

Amanda Wilson (7)
Oxgangs Primary School

Football

I play football at break time at school,
Kenan is best at it in my class
And I am the best goalkeeper they've ever had,
Sometimes I score, sometimes I don't
And I can't dribble the ball for very long,
A boy called Andrew is the same as me
And I get very, very dirty.

Adam Murphy (7)
Oxgangs Primary School

Back In Time

I want to go back in time,
I want to see the knights,
My brain is full of things,
I thought of going to see a castle,
I think I will be a knight,
You must think it is impossible,
It is not impossible, it is good.

Struan Sloan (7)
Oxgangs Primary School

We Are All Different

Black skin or white skin
Dark hair or fair
Blue, brown or green eyes
Boy or a girl
You are who you are
If you wear skirts or dresses
Trousers or shorts
Short sleeves or long sleeves
Vest tops or crop tops
High-heeled shoes or no heels
Boots, trainers or sandals
You are who you are
We are all different
That's what makes life exciting
You are a star whoever you are
So let's stop racism.

Briony O'Keefe (9)
Oxgangs Primary School

It Is Boring Being A Snake

It is boring being a snake
Slithering along doing nothing
It is boring slithering along all day
And that is why I'm moaning

It is boring being a snake
And I don't like any cake
So when it comes to my birthday
I just slither to the lake.

Adam Weir (9)
Oxgangs Primary School

Little Mouse

Oh dear little mouse please come out,
I want to be friends,
I'll give you fresh water every day
And buy you a mini bed,
Oh please little mouse please come out.

Oh dear little mouse please come out,
You don't have to live in that hole,
I'll ask my mum if I can keep you,
I'll even ask my dad to build you a luxurious home,
Oh please little mouse please come out.

Oh dear little mouse please come out,
I'll give you any food you want,
A piece of wood to sharpen your teeth,
Oh please little mouse please come out.

PS: Mouse's reply, *I'll sleep on it.*

Nadia Hussain (9)
Oxgangs Primary School

Funky Cow

Funky cow fly around
Funky cow touch the ground

Funky cow do the kung fu
Funky cow do the loo

Funky cow do gymnastics
Funky cow play with elastics

PS: The funkiest cow in the world.

Yasmin Rasul (9)
Oxgangs Primary School

Hands And Feet

Stepping in the mud,
Sliding on the ice,
Tripping over rocks.

Swinging on the monkey bars,
Pushing the ball over the volleyball net,
Bouncing a basketball,
Catching a cricket ball,
Saving a football that's flying through the air,
Mucking about with a football,
Swimming in the sea,
Running a couple of miles.

Getting blisters
And varicose veins,
Breaking or stubbing fingers and toes.

Putting on shoes
Or socks
Or even slippers.

Driving a car, taxi, bus
Or even a motorbike.

Stroking pets,
Gently stroking a hamster,
Carefully feeding fish.

I bet people wouldn't buy pets if they had no hands
And you can't do any of that without hands and feet.

Alex Cork (11)
Oxgangs Primary School

My Life As A Pencil

I sit on the table as usual,
Then I write a letter to my owner's friend
And she is called Sarah,
Then I write another letter to her friend, Kirsty.

Emily Youngs (7)
Oxgangs Primary School

Choccy

'Mammy, Mammy, can I go buy some choccy?
A big Dairy Milk or some mint poppies,
Mouth-drooling nougat or a big cube of toffee,
Mammy, Mammy, can I go buy some choccy?'

'Oh you can't buy any choccy, Son, I'll tell ya that!
Your disgusting drool is falling on the cat,
No toffee, no poppies, no mouth-drooling sweets,
You don't deserve any nice treats!'

'But Mammy, there's a sale on at the corner shops
And it's only 5p for a pack of pops,
I know I'm not nice and very naughty,
But please Mammy, can I go buy some choccy?'

'No, no, no, I'm not taking anymore,
No more choccy or out that door,
You are going to be stuffed with treats,
You can have anything except a bag of sweets!'

'Mammy please let me eat,
Just one little sweet,
I'm a chocoholic so I am,
So I'll make my own sweet in the frying pan!'

'I don't understand you are so weird,
You'll be begging me till you grow a beard,
Actually I fancy some poppies,
OK Son, go buy some choccy!'

'Mammy, Mammy, I love choccy!'

Nicola Peat (10)
Oxgangs Primary School

Poor Daft Dugs

A daft dug has a hairy wame,
They run like mad,
Oh what a shame,
They woof all night
And cry all day,
The poor things are even left as strays,
Dugs can be cute (some people say),
But I think they're daft 'cause they run away,
They sniff with their noses day after day,
But people still like them, *'Why?'* I say,
They have very good hearing,
But that's because of their lugs,
They always knock over plates and jugs,
I've just seen a dug who looks lonely and is a stray,
He looked really sad, 'Poor dug,' I say,
I've taken this dug to the vet and she says,
'Can you look after him every day?'
. . . 'Yes,' I say.

Carly Burnett (9)
Oxgangs Primary School

The Adventure Of My Nose

My nose is sore when bumped or banged,
My nose is tickly when just sneezed,
My nose bleeds after picking,
If you have a nose you could smell your mum's cheesy feet,
The smell of bacon flying into my nostrils,
The warning to wake up.

Scott Wilson (12)
Oxgangs Primary School

Big Sister

Mum, I've always wanted a big sister,
What about you Mum?
Your hair is sleek and shiny,
Your clothes are cool!
Mum, you rule!

We could go to the shops,
We could buy lollipops,
We could buy slippers
And read the book 'Shivers',
Be my sister, Mum!

We could go to the swimming pool
And always skip school,
Let's go and buy new shoes
And then I think we should have a snooze.

Could we go and buy a light
Then have a pillow fight?
Then we will go to bed
Or camp out by the shed,
Oh Mum, be my big sister.

Sarah Hunter (10)
Oxgangs Primary School

Cat

I have a cat
That can read and write,
That can play football,
That can watch TV at night,
She can talk like a human
And she is also very brainy,
She likes to run and play
When it is rainy.

Leigh Innes (7)
Oxgangs Primary School

The Months Of The Year

You may think that months are quite boring
But they are really jazzy and cool
They make the year change away
This is all their names

There's jazzy January and funky February
There's moving and grooving March
Have I told you about amazing April
Or marvellous May?

How could I forget about jumping June
Oh yeah jolly July and awesome August
Also super September
Or outstanding October

I love all the months
But there are just two more and they are
Noisy November
And dancing December.

Eleanor Campbell (10)
Oxgangs Primary School

Sunny Days

Sunny days are the best
We skip and dance around and around
When it is time to go in, we are sad
In the morning we are happy
And go out to play.

Molly Meikle (7)
Oxgangs Primary School

What My Feet Do

My feet are always busy
Whether it's stamping in mud
Or kicking a ball in the back of the net
They always seem to be kept busy!

My feet have to be dragged to school every morning
They love to help me run though
They trudge through the snow on a cold winter's night
They slide on slippery ice
They do so much, it amazes me how they have the energy

My feet are glad when it comes to bedtime
They finally get to breathe as I take off my shoes and socks
Sometimes they are still moving when I am asleep
As I wake up they are ready for another day of fun.

Grant Clark (11)
Oxgangs Primary School

Hands

My hands are cool,
they slap and they pull,
they also touch and feel.
My hands are cool,
they slap and they pull,
no one can take them
because they're my hands.
My hands are cool,
they slap and they pull,
my hands are cool,
they can pick up lots of items.
My hands are cool,
they slap and pull.

Carrie Smith (11)
Oxgangs Primary School

It's Time They Got Some Thanks!

My feet amaze me,
They are just totally crazy,
Running, jumping, dancing, prancing,
They do it all the time,
I think it's time they got some thanks.

They are quite often in pain,
But they are still insane,
Pedalling, kicking, walking, racing,
They know it off by heart,
Don't you think it's time they got a bit of space.

They don't often jerk,
Still they always go berserk,
Splashing, dashing, speeding, booting,
They do it without needing to be told,
We think it's time they got a bit of fun.

They hardly ever need mended,
Even though they are demented,
Hopping, skipping, trudging, pushing,
It's impossible to fake,
They need some recognition.

They never ever stick,
Even though they are frantic,
Slipping, swinging, sliding, marching,
You sit back and let them do their job,
It's time they got some thanks!

Euan Ballantyne (11)
Oxgangs Primary School

Pencil Sharpener

I am a pencil sharpener
I hate it when people put pencils in their mouth
I hate being a pencil sharpener!
Sigh.

Natty Clark (7)
Oxgangs Primary School

Nose

Noses have a hard life
They smell bad things
But also good things like cooked
Bacon and sausages
Noses also breathe
And sneeze
They sometimes change
Colour and life.

Kyle Adamson (10)
Oxgangs Primary School

The School

I am the school,
I hardly sleep.
When the alarm goes beep, beep, beep,
When the lights go on in the morning,
I know when the teacher is here,
As sharp as a spear.
I groan when she shouts
And the children moan,
But when they've gone and I'm all alone,
It's very quiet and peaceful.
Until my enemy, the alarm, goes off again,
Sigh . . . I have to get ready for another day
And that's me,
The school.

Emily Mann (10)
Palnackie Primary School

Leaf

I am a leaf,
I perch on my branch up high,
Taller than any house.

I do not have anywhere special to go,
So I drift,
In the cool breeze.

I whisper,
In the wind,
I hold secrets that only I can tell.

People have no respect for me,
I was quietly whispering to Mrs Acorn and I was bewildered
By the banging from below.

The unrooted ones
Were hammering a basketball ring
Into my dear friend,
Mr Trunk.

And when autumn comes,
I slowly lower,
To the ground.

And me, Mrs Leafy, Mr Cackleberry, Miss Tapster and Sir Longland
Are all raked up and thrown about and stood on
And put in a big black tub.
And there I stay,

Until I am used for soil
And dirt,
And never noticed.

Molly Irving (10)
Palnackie Primary School

A Fly

I am a fly,
Oh why, oh why does everyone hate a fly?
Every day of my life is a struggle to survive,
With newspapers trying to hit me and everyone stamping and
trampling on me
Nobody wants to hug me or stroke me or want me as a pet
But there is one advantage to being a fly
Getting to listen in on all the gossip!
One day we flies will gain our revenge and
Take over the world!

Lucy Niven
Palnackie Primary School

My Christmas Poem

On Christmas morning,
I touch the colourful wrapping paper,
I taste the lovely turkey,
I see the shiny ribbons,
I smell the Christmas pudding,
I hear Santa's footsteps,
I feel excited.

Tom Niven (9)
Palnackie Primary School

My Christmas Poem

I touch my presents
I taste Christmas pudding
I see sleigh marks
I smell the Christmas tree
I hear hooves
I feel happiness.

Fraser Firth (8)
Palnackie Primary School

A Piece Of Paper

If I was a piece of paper,
I'd be lovely and shiny,
I would be in the writing caper.

I'd have an A+ essay written on me,
A frame around my sides
And my writer would have an award-winning prize!

Chloe Ellis (11)
Palnackie Primary School

Writing

Writing is boring
Writing is rubbish
We do it every week
It's writing a story
Or writing a poem
Or even a letter
Lines and lines of stupid writing
It is really quite boring
If you know what I mean
The clock drags by
When we're doing writing
I wish I was home helping my dad
But I'm in school doing writing.

Callum Park (10)
Sanquhar Primary School

The Poor Boy

The little poor boy sits in his house,
Instead of counting sheep it's rats or a mouse,
He has lots of brothers and sisters, actually nine,
He was worked since he was six, down the mine.
He watches in envy as the posh boys go for a holiday,
He would love to go to school but he can't, no way.
He is fed up with life, so he packs his bags,
Well, it's a hanky tied to a stick,
With a hat, trousers and a scarf in good nick,
His mother hasn't time to go looking, so she cries,
But she has lots more, so she wipes her eyes.
The boy goes over the misty hill,
He tries to find shelter because of the chill,
He thought he would be happy but that didn't work,
He isn't any happier in the city with all the posh people.
He tries to get into the big posh house,
Now he can't complain, not a mouse.
It is perfect, like nothing he has seen,
On the table a lot of food and greens.
He takes it outside and has a grand old feast,
He actually looks fatter but not obese.
Oh no! The chicken was raw,
But he had eaten it jaw to jaw.
He went to sleep with a tummy ache,
He slept and slept but didn't awake.
He was lying on a flowerbed,
He had a smile on his face,
A great grin on his head,
For once he is happy although he is dead.

Isabel Gordon (10)
Sanquhar Primary School

I Hate School!

I hate school you always have to work your best,
The teachers never let you take a rest,
I hate school you never can disobey the rules,
All the popular girls think they're cool,
I hate school!

When you go to school you always get a row,
All that's there is maths, spelling and English now,
I really, really hate writing,
When you go outside, someone is always fighting,
I hate school!

Mind you, PE is not so bad,
When you run like mad,
But PE goes by fast,
It never does last,
I hate school!

When someone takes a tantrum,
The teacher starts to rant,
School is so boring,
All the teachers think they're the king,
I hate school!

Brenna Aston (10)
Sanquhar Primary School

My Class

Emma - she is annoying, she keeps talking and I can't get
                                              on with my work
Neil - he gets a pencil and pretends to smoke it
Claire - she bites her nails and doesn't stop until home time
Brenda - she talks to Claire and doesn't share
Miss White - she's always right, she goes outside and gets a fright
Rhys - he sits at a table on his own, he does his work and sings a tune
Daniel - he's got muscles, weights, he lifts them every night
Scott - tries his best but he's a pest
Murray - he eats some curry for his lunch
Coral - always has a chat and her teacher comes and pats
                                              her on the back
Leigh - gets grumpy when Calum annoys her
Jason - when we do maths Jason says he's got a sore head.

Ben Waugh (10)
Sanquhar Primary School

Super Gran

My gran is a super gran, she dances up the street,
She whizzes through the shop so fast you wouldn't see her feet.
She wears the latest football strips, she wears all the
                                              most fashionable clothes,
She would love to be a supermodel and do the coolest pose.
She wants to live in Hollywood and go meet all the stars,
She would love to be a spaceman and travel up to Mars.
She's got her own PlayStation 2, she plays it all the time,
My gran is a super gran and she's aged 69.
My gran eats lots of junk food, especially lots of sweets,
She gives me lots of presents and a lot of treats.
I love my gran, she's a super gran, I play with her a lot,
But when she can't be bothered, she sits on her lazy bot.

Leigh Clark (10)
Sanquhar Primary School

Yu-Gi-Oh!

The Blue Eyes White Dragon's proud roar
Against Korbo's galore,
The Dark Magician's flash
Against the Buster Blader's slash,
Strike Ninja's speed
Is very good indeed,
Firegrass is a weed,
You don't need.
Dark Paladin's magic slash
Will send a monster to the trash,
Then he drew it,
The card of destiny,
The card of fate,
But it was too late,
No one could whine,
It was just a matter of time.

Colin Baird (10)
Sanquhar Primary School

When I Watched Grease

I was lying in my bed watching TV,
Watching my new tape, Grease,
Like Sandy and Danny and the Pink Ladies,
Because they are the best.
I wish I could act in a film like Grease,
Be famous and be on TV.
On my 10th birthday my pals dressed up,
As people out of Grease.
I was just at the bit where they were going to kiss
And my mum shouted up, 'Coral, dinner's ready.'
I turned off the TV and went downstairs,
Ran downstairs in a mood,
Hated my dinner but ate it up
And said, 'Mum, that was good.'

Coral Anderson (10)
Sanquhar Primary School

Playground Fun

Smack! It's another goal
Ten-nil, you are the best
Goal, goal, goal

He wouldn't stop, slide, slice
Another pass, run, *run,* goal
13-nil, two minutes left
Let's get another goal
Beep, beep, time out

Another good game and passing
Now to winter

Squeeze, squeeze, squeeze throw
Smack right on the head
Ow, I'll get you
Next day

Squeeze, squeeze, lob, smack
Crack a window
Now that had a stone in it

Run, run, run, leg it, hide
He's out
Lob
Smack! Ha ha, got him
Right in the face
But the window
£100 out of pocket.

Neil Moffat (10)
Sanquhar Primary School

Football

Football is fun
Football is for everyone
It doesn't matter is you're different
It doesn't matter if you're disabled
It doesn't matter if you smell or reek
Everyone's good at football
If you are a famous footballer
You're no better than the rest
Everyone's just the best
I feel sorry for the Scottish football team
They never win a thing
But I always will support them through everything
Whatever the result
Most of the boys like it, especially me
My favourite footballer is Stefan Klos
The goalkeeper for Rangers
I like him the best.

Brendan Moore (10)
Sanquhar Primary School

Music

When I play the piano or shout or sing,
Something happens to me, a wonderful thing,
The beat starts to jingle, my voice starts to tingle,
I feel as if I'm a superstar.
I can feel a difference in my usual way
And I play and play and play.
Suddenly I'm in front of loads of people,
I'm wearing the most fashionable clothes,
I dance my grooviest, funkiest dance,
I run around the stage, people cheering at me,
Then, 'Rachel, it's time for tea!'

Rachel Wilson (10)
Sanquhar Primary School

Swimming Pool

I get my swimming trunks on
And jump in the pool
Then I splash my friends
And swim up to the deep end
Down the green flume
Flashing and splashing
Swimming is fun for everyone.

Kieran McCusker
St Joseph's RC Primary School, Stranraer

Best Friends

Best friends
Friends care for you
They pick you up when you fall
When you are sad or unhappy
They will cheer you up
Friends are the best thing in the world.

Jade McCulloch (8)
St Joseph's RC Primary School, Stranraer

Fruit

F ive is the amount you should eat every day
R ipe when it is ready to eat
U mpteen different varieties
I ncredibly delicious, so munch, munch away
T omatoes, tangerines to name just two.

Stacy Paterson (10)
St Joseph's RC Primary School, Stranraer

Playground

P eople playing
L oving having fun in the sun
A nd people running in the playground
Y ou are being with your friends
G oing all around the place
R unning around the playground
O thers walking about
U p and down the steps
N early bell time
D own the stairs outside.

Lauren Lowe (9)
St Joseph's RC Primary School, Stranraer

Too Late

I was going to skate but it was too late
I was going to the park but it was too dark
I was going to the shops to buy plenty
But found my pockets were empty
Too late, too dark, too empty and tomorrow will be plenty.

Amber Feeney (7)
St Joseph's RC Primary School, Stranraer

Pool

My favourite game is pool
I play it sometimes after school
I think it is really cool
It is better than playing in a swimming pool.

Elliot Monaghan (7)
St Joseph's RC Primary School, Stranraer

Playground

P laying in the playground
L ots of running around
A ll having lots of fun
Y es, I can skip
G irls chase the boys
R ound and round
O ver the ball goes
U p and down
N early bell time
D oor tightly shut.

Heather Corrigan (9)
St Joseph's RC Primary School, Stranraer

Sun And Moon

Playing in the sun
My brother and I have loads of fun
When we see the moon
We know it's time for home soon
When the stars are shining bright
We know it's time to say goodnight.

Kiera Hilton (7)
St Joseph's RC Primary School, Stranraer

There Was A Boy From Belfast

There was a boy from Belfast
Who went to an English class
The teacher was rude
And very crude
But in his test he passed.

Matthew Love (8)
St Joseph's RC Primary School, Stranraer

Limerick

There was a young man from Dumfries
He thought about joining the police
First he was sad
Then he was glad
Because he found out he could help keep the peace.

Rachel Drysdale (8)
St Joseph's RC Primary School, Stranraer

Young Man From Ukraine

There was a young man from Ukraine
Who really hated the rain
He had a big hat
In which lived a rat
Who loved doing dances from Spain.

Gregor Feeney (9)
St Joseph's RC Primary School, Stranraer

Tractors

Dirty big wheels,
Strong big working machines,
Fun to watch and a bumpy ride,
Tractors.

Fergus Lochhead (8)
St Joseph's RC Primary School, Stranraer

Funtair

Far along the road
Under the sun
Near the apple tree
The funfair was about to begin
Air blowing this way and that
In and around the trees
Running to the rides just like leaves
Twirling upside-down, spinning round and round
Running with excitement, oh what fun!
Then I had candyfloss
Lots of sweets too
Tired now, lots of fun
Slowly now the day is done.

Chelsea Westran (9)
St Joseph's RC Primary School, Stranraer

Jennifer

J ennifer, Jennifer, that's my name
E veryone wants me to play their game
N ever, never nasty
N early always kind
I ce cream, ice cream is what I like
F riends I play with on my bike
E xercising, exercising is good for me
R eading in the library, you have to be quiet.

Jennifer McCusker (9)
St Joseph's RC Primary School, Stranraer

I Spy

I spy a cottage
With a straw thatched roof.
I spy a butterfly
With different coloured spots.
I spy a reindeer
Flying through the air.
I spy the stars
Shining in the dark.
I spy the sun
With an orange warm centre.
I spy a spaceship
With a man inside.
I spy you
Laughing and giggling.

Poppy Arkless (9)
St Joseph's RC Primary School, Stranraer

Go-Kart

I have a go-kart, its engine is noisy
When I spin the wheels get mossy
Round and round the track we go
The rev counters going high and low
I hit a bump and bit my lips
Oops! I just spun into the chips
Hooray, I got first place
Which means I am ace.

Kyle McCulloch (10)
St Joseph's RC Primary School, Stranraer

I'm Richer Than You

My daddy's richer than your daddy
And I've got a better car too,
My mummy's posher than your mum,
That makes me better than you!

My room is bigger than yours
And I have a nicer piano too,
My toys are more fun that your toys,
I'm so much better than you!

My house is more fun that yours
And I have more animals too,
My TV is louder than your TV,
That makes me better than you.

My daddy's richer than your dad,
But you've got a better car too,
Your mummy's posher than my mum,
That makes me the same as you!

Samantha Henderson (10)
St Joseph's RC Primary School, Stranraer

Animals At Night

Owls at night their eyes shine bright
Gives a hoot, oh what a fright!
In the trees snuggled up tight
Waiting for their night-time flight

Moles come out of their holes to spy
Furry creatures go rushing by
The fox with his red coat gleaming in the moonlight
Howling and whining in the snow so bright

Cats go out on their nightly haunt
To catch a mouse that they want
As the dawn begins, the sky starts to clear
The animals start to disappear.

Jeri-Ann Mulligan (10)
St Joseph's RC Primary School, Stranraer

The Castle

I've decided I'll go out for a walk
I turned around and looked at my clock
I don't care if it's late at night
The dark does not give me a fright
Sneak out the door, make sure you're quiet
There's a cat just tiptoed by it

I saw a castle, I hadn't seen it before
I had an idea, I went to explore
As I got closer the castle walls got taller
I looked behind, my house was much smaller
I had walked miles but I was there at last
If I wanted a good look I better be fast
Around the castle was a moat
The only way across was by boat

Luckily around the moat I saw
A boat that's name is Devil's Jaw
It was red and the writing was gold
By the rust and the rot I could tell it was old
I found an old raft, it was green and blue
But it started to sink, *not you too!*

I'd better get home, the sun is rising
Shouted a man, 'You shouldn't be guising'
I finally got home and jumped into bed
Half an hour later my mum touched my head
'It's morning darling,' she said with a yawn
I looked out the window and the castle was gone.

Robert Mackenzie (10)
St Joseph's RC Primary School, Stranraer

When I'm Bigger

When I'm bigger I want to be
A teacher
In fact I'd rather be
A model
No, actually
A pop star
Maybe I'll be
An astronaut

When I'm bigger I want to live
In a bungalow,
No, too big
A flat
No, too little
Or a caravan
No, not that sturdy
Or maybe I'll just stick with a house

When I'm bigger I want to drive
A big red car
No, I don't like red
Or a sports car
No, too small
No, actually a motorbike
Yeah!

Shannan Corrigan (11)
St Joseph's RC Primary School, Stranraer

Rose!

There once was a girl called Rose
Who had a very big nose
She said, 'I don't lie
I didn't eat that pie'
But her nose grew as long as a hose.

Iona Donnelly (11)
St Joseph's RC Primary School, Stranraer

Close Your Eyes

Close your eyes
What can you see in your dream?
Maybe a lamb or some trees

Close your eyes
Look, there's a bird and butterfly
What colour are they?
Are they red, green, blue, silver or black?

Close your eyes
And look deeply into yourself
And can you see a soldier or drummer boy?

Close your eyes
And look carefully
Can you see teachers
Or can you see friends?

Close your eyes
Imagine you are going to work
On a plane or bus
Just close your eyes.

Karina McCusker (10)
St Joseph's RC Primary School, Stranraer

Jenette's Pets!

There once was a girl called Jenette
Who had a very strange pet
It sat on her rug
Drank from a jug
And then it took off like a jet.

Gina Soriani (11)
St Joseph's RC Primary School, Stranraer

Ode Tae Sausages

Sausages, sausages, all kinds of sausages
There are so many of you sausages
You can get hot dogs
Chilli dogs
And cheesy dogs
And sometimes with mustard
But never with custard

You are round
And you are brown
You sizzle and spit away in your pan
Hot with chips
And cold with dips
I like you with beans
But not with greens!

Every snorker
Is a corker
I like batter
On my Frankfurter
I like you in sausage rolls
And also in toad in the holes

You can get Lorne sossies
And lean bangers
I like you grilled
Or reheated
I don't mind if you're thick
I don't mind if you're thin
I don't mind if you're fat
I don't mind if you're short

I don't care if you're a Cumberland sausage
I don't care if people call you snags
You'll still be sausages to me!

Andrew Bull (10)
St Mary's Music School, Edinburgh

Chocolate

1 bar of chocolate
I like so much
I peel off the wrapping
I have a munch
It's very tasty, tasty chocolate
I like every kind
It melts in my mouth

I'd eat it in a house
I'd eat it with a mouse
I'd eat it in a boat
I'd eat it with a goat
Until I go pop
Until I explode
Until I go fizzing down the road
Melting gooey tasty chocolate.

Kieran Baker (9)
St Mary's Music School, Edinburgh

Sunny Days

Sunny days are the best days,
They're the best because they are warm and bright,
Sunny days, sunny days.

Sunny days are the best days,
Especially the best when the flowers bloom,
Sunny days, sunny days.

Sunny days are the best days,
When the bees and butterflies come out to play,
Sunny days, sunny days.

Sunny days are the best days,
Even when the warm showers come,
Sunny days, sunny days.

Sunny days are the best days,
The best days because they're my days.

Caitlin Spencer (10)
St Mary's Music School, Edinburgh

The Farmer's Rescue

One young piglet,
Lifeless, cold
And perished.

Icy wind, rain slashed,
An eye not open,
A smooth black body,
Without clean straw bed.

A tail, long, straight,
Not curled or wound,
Nor twisted or spiralled.

Body soft,
Concrete hard,
Still no move,
But yet . . .

For luck, for heart
And a work roughed hand,
Scoops down, down . . .

Curled and warmed,
Shiny and smooth,
A touch of a back,
A squeak and squeal.

Two sets of teeth,
A prick like a needle,
A sore sharp pain.

A nose like rubber,
Snuffles through straw,
A comfort of a sow,
A great warm mother!

Alice Burn (11)
St Mary's Music School, Edinburgh

In A Poem

My favourite times are when the
Sky is blue and snowy-white,
Accompanied by a gleam of
Restless flickering light.
When you enter a poem
Your background seems to change
Into a living form of magic
That you simply can't arrange.
Nothing in it stands out
But shows their form of light.
Until the darkness shadows
Like late evening in the night.
You feel a chill of sunless dull
Run down your spine
And feel this place's beauty
Run in later time.
Until the sun returns and the sky is blue
Some more,
You feel again that heavenly
Gleaming sky will colour pour,
Lovely blue and icy cloudy snow,
Waiting for the sunshine to finish off its glow.

Katherine Carr (9)
St Mary's Music School, Edinburgh

Dark

In the park, in the dark, on your own,
There might be something waiting to lurch out,
A monster with killer teeth!
A poisoned bee!
A deadly tree!
You never know what happens in the *dark!*

Chiara Margiotta (8)
St Mary's RC Primary School, Bonnyrigg

If

If I were a cat
I'd like
A lovely new hat

If I were a snake
I'd like
A huge brake

If I were a rabbit
I'd like
A good carrot

If I were a lizard
I'd like
A big blizzard

If I were a daring dog
I'd like
A good jog.

Shaun Muir (8)
St Mary's RC Primary School, Bonnyrigg

Wishes

I wish I was a shark
Swimming in the sea.

I wish I was a horse
Riding on the path.

I wish I was a cat
Climbing up the wall.

I wish I was a rabbit
Diving into the bush.

Paul Brogan (8)
St Mary's RC Primary School, Bonnyrigg

If

If I were a cat
I'd want
A ginger rat!

If I were a rabbit
I'd want
To get rid of the habit!

If I were a snake
I'd want
To bake a cake!

If I were a lizard
I'd want
To be a wizard!

But as a really fat pig
I want
To be extremely big.

Ashleigh MacFeate (8)
St Mary's RC Primary School, Bonnyrigg

Wishes

I wish I was a princess
So I could ride on a pretty carriage.

I wish I was a mermaid
So I could swim around the sea.

I wish I was a kitten
So I could climb and curl in my master's lap.

I wish I was a puppy
So I could wander around the garden.

Adriane Napa (8)
St Mary's RC Primary School, Bonnyrigg

If

If I were a rabbit
I'd like
A long, long carrot!

If I were a cat
I'd like
A very new hat!

If I were a snake
I'd like
To make a cake!

If I were a lizard
I'd like
To be a dizzy wizard!

But as a dizzy dog
I like
To walk through some fog.

Gemma Smith (8)
St Mary's RC Primary School, Bonnyrigg

Wishes

I wish I had a dolphin
So I could ride on it all day.
I wish I could have my own swimming pool,
I could swim in it every morning and night.
I wish I could be a princess
So I could stroll along the park.
I wish I had two puppies,
I would play with them all day.

Rosie Jones (8)
St Mary's RC Primary School, Bonnyrigg

If

If I were a rose
I'd want
To have a big blue nose!

If I were a daisy
I'd want
To be a little big lazy!

If I were a bush
I'd want
A little push!

If I were a tree
I'd want
A big green bee!

But as a stripy sunflower
I'd want
A lot of power!

Hannah Brosnan (8)
St Mary's RC Primary School, Bonnyrigg

ABC

A B C
I am hiding from a bee
D E F G
There it is, can you see?
H I J K
It went away
L M N O
Which way did it go?
P Q R
It has gone too far
S T U V
There it was with another bee
W X Y Z
Now I can go to bed.

Erin Devine (8)
St Mary's RC Primary School, Bonnyrigg

Bee Up A Tree

A B C
I saw a bumblebee
D E F G
Flee up a tree
H I J K
Playing in a honeycomb
L M N O
And said no!
P Q R
It's too far
S T U V
He looked at a star
W X Y Z
And went to bed.

Rachael Douglas (8)
St Mary's RC Primary School, Bonnyrigg

Who Am I?

I'm the sort of person who likes to play with my sister
I'm the sort of person who hates to laugh
Happiness for me is school
Frightening for me is spiders
I'm the sort of person who imagines that there are
Ghosts in my room
I'm the sort of person who wants to fly
I dream that one day I'll be a hairdresser
But for now I'm just normal.

Diana McLaren (8)
St Mary's RC Primary School, Bonnyrigg

Who Am I?

I'm the sort of person who likes to watch EastEnders
I'm the sort of person who hates to watch Coronation Street
Happiness for me is playing with my friends
Frightening for me is when the windows slam at night
I'm the sort of person who imagines living in a paradise
I'm the sort of person who wants to be a millionaire
I dream that one day I'll be married to a prince
But for now I'm just a perfect girl.

Clara Fraser (8)
St Mary's RC Primary School, Bonnyrigg

Who Am I?

I'm the sort of person who likes to play
I'm the sort of person who hates to be alone
Happiness for me is my family
Frightening for me is vampires
I'm the sort of person who imagines a crocodile is in my bed
I'm the sort of person who wants my great granny
I dream that one day I'll be an artist
But for now I'm just alone.

Islay Coppola (8)
St Mary's RC Primary School, Bonnyrigg

Who Am I?

I'm the sort of person who likes to watch Coronation Street
I'm the sort of person who hates to watch EastEnders
Happiness for me is playing with my friends
Frightening for me is when it is dark
I'm the sort of person who imagines I'm in Sweety Land
I'm the sort of person who wants all the money in the world
I dream that one day I'll get married to a prince
But for now I'm just a sweety pie.

Hayley Wilson (8)
St Mary's RC Primary School, Bonnyrigg

If

If I were a pig
I'd want
To dig something big!

If I were a snake
I'd want
To bake a cake!

If I were a lizard
I'd want
To be a magical wizard!

If I were a cow
I'd want
To take a bow!

But as a big fat cat
I want
A nice wiggly hat!

Erin Brolly (8)
St Mary's RC Primary School, Bonnyrigg

Wishes

I wish I had a horse
So I can ride on it

I wish I had a kitten
So it can wander in the house

I wish I had a bunny
So I can feed it

I wish I had a dolphin
So I can swim in the water.

Carly Gulland (8)
St Mary's RC Primary School, Bonnyrigg

If

If I were a monkey
I'd be
Really funky!

If I were a cat
I'd be
Oh so fat!

If I were a lizard
I'd be
A pinball wizard!

If I were a snake
I'd be
Eating a coco-flake!

But as a crazy turkey
I'd go
Clurky clurky!

Kyle Wilson (8)
St Mary's RC Primary School, Bonnyrigg

Who Am I?

I'm the sort of person who likes to be good
I'm the sort of person who hates to go to school
Happiness for me is going places
Frightening for me is fun
I'm the sort of person who imagines my mum wouldn't be too moany
I'm the sort of person who wants blue hair
I dream that one day I'll like school
But for now I'm just bored.

Sean Thomson (8)
St Mary's RC Primary School, Bonnyrigg

If

If I were a star
I'd dream
That I could have a pink car

If I were the moon
I'd dream
That my birthday is soon

If I were the sun
I'd dream
That I was cool and fun

If I were Mars
I'd dream
That I'd have lots of cars

But as the sky
I dream
That I could lie.

Shannon McAra (8)
St Mary's RC Primary School, Bonnyrigg

Who Am I?

I'm the sort of person who likes to play football
I'm the sort of person who hates to go to school
Happiness for me is getting presents
Frightening for me is my house, haunted
I'm the sort of person who imagines I have head lice
I'm the sort of person who wants to be a footballer
I dream that one day I'll be a famous racer
But for now I'm just a person.

Mark Kean (8)
St Mary's RC Primary School, Bonnyrigg

If

If I were a snake
I'd hate
To get hit with a rake!

If I were a lizard
I'd hate
To eat a wizard!

If I were a dog
I'd hate
To smell a bog!

If I were a cat
I'd hate
A new hat!

But as a jungle croc
I'd hate
To eat a smelly sock.

Steven Gilmour (8)
St Mary's RC Primary School, Bonnyrigg

Wishes

I wish I was a dragon
So I could blow fire out my mouth

I wish I could fly
And zoom through the sky

I wish I was a tyrannosaurus rex
I'd say, 'I am big!'

I wish I were a wizard
So I could have a mince pie!

Daniel Morrison (8)
St Mary's RC Primary School, Bonnyrigg

Who Am I?

I'm the sort of person who likes to play football
I'm the sort of person who hates to fight
Happiness for me is having a new Ranger's strip
Frightening for me is my sister
I'm the sort of person who imagines being on Mars
I'm the sort of person who wants to be rich
I dream that one day I'll be good
But for now I'm just me.

Stewart Brown (8)
St Mary's RC Primary School, Bonnyrigg

The Wardrobe

I am a wardrobe
I've got two eyes
I really smell of wood
I am very messy inside

A full bucket of rubbish all over the floor
A stinky bedroom not getting tidied
A big load of pens not getting used
And a pair of smelly socks
A white fluffy cat toy lying on the floor

A pink fluffy coat
A pair of dirty damp trainers
And a denim notebook all ripped and tattered
I can see a chess game with no pieces only a board and a box
A pair of wellies on the bottom.

Natasha Cumming (8)
Stobhill Primary School

The Wardrobe

I am a wardrobe
I am a dusty old wardrobe

Smelly shoes on the floor
Food under the bed
Green wallpaper
Dirty pants

Games and clothes to be tidied up
A ripped sun hat waiting to be sewed
A glove resting for the winter
Money on the top secret place
Coats that are too small.

Sean McColm (8)
Stobhill Primary School

The Wardrobe

I am a wardrobe
I am untidy inside

I can see shiny shoes under the bed
And junk under the desk
Ripped teddies under the covers
Hats and glasses on the windowsill
I can see bed pillows on the floor

I am a nasty wardrobe that has a nasty smell
I am a tall wardrobe
I have two circles on my front
I can see toys over the floor
I can see a grizzly cat on the bed.

Kimberley Rice (8)
Stobhill Primary School

The Wardrobe

I am a wardrobe
I smell nice
I've got two eyes
I can see inside and outside

A big bed waiting for the boy
Cars to get played with
A computer to get typed on
A PS2 to play on

Jeans for a party
Football strip for the next match
Sunglasses and a baseball hat for the summer
A good shirt waiting for a party invitation
Jogging bottoms for sports day.

Kyle Fleming (8)
Stobhill Primary School

The Wardrobe

I am a wardrobe
I've got two eyes
I smell of lovely perfume inside

I see clothes that need to be put away
Teddy in the bed
A little girl having a party
A bed that's not been made
Teddies scattered on the floor making a massive mess
Baby rattles under the bed

Cosy jammies so fluffy and pink
Sparkly clothes for fancy parties
Fancy tops so beautiful and shimmery
Jeans for playing outside.

Natalie Cumming (8)
Stobhill Primary School

The Wardrobe

I am a wardrobe
I've got two eyes
I can see outside and inside

Smelly clothes on the floor
A little girl is playing with her best friend
Sparkly shoes on the floor
The white fluffy cat is curled up on the bed
The curtains are so smelly that I cannot look at them

Party clothes waiting for an invitation
Furry coats waiting for winter to come
Knee-high boots for a great party
The little girl's slippers for wearing at night-time
Sparkly shoes for a disco
Sparkly dresses for going to a school party
Sparkly make-up waiting for parties and discos.

Chloe Birrell (8)
Stobhill Primary School

The Wardrobe

I am a wardrobe
I have two big eyes
I can see outside and inside

I can see a scared cat sitting under the bed
I can see scuffed boots
I can see a dog going in the bath
I can see socks lying about
I can see a nice coat waiting for winter

I can see two naughty girls messing up their bedroom
I can see a fish.

Amy Cornwall (8)
Stobhill Primary School

The Wardrobe

I am a wardrobe
I am brown
I'm old and scruffy
I've got two eyes
I can see outside and inside
I smell really good

Scraped old cards on the sturdy old carpet
I can see a nice new bunk bed
PlayStation 1 with tonnes of games around it

Christmas jeans waiting for a Christmas invitation
Gloves snoozing until the winter
Football strip crushed at the bottom
Sun hats ready for the summer.

Glenn Ross (8)
Stobhill Primary School

Space Journey

In my silver steel shuttle spaceship
Soaring into space
Comets coming closer
I avoid meteoroids and asteroids
And the searing sun
Shimmering shooting stars
Zoom by my eyes.

Sophie Graham (9)
The Mary Erskine & Stewart's Melville Junior School

Solar Space

The magical, metallic planet Mars
Like a crashing, crackling crater
Red, rocky and rusty landscape
Leave the little planets till later

NASA probes pursuing patiently
Beagle bust and blown away
Scientists studying swirling stars
Tactfully tackling terrific Mars

Pluto coldest, crackling planet
As cold as icy igloo seas
Secretive, skyless planet
Blue as wondrous, wonderful seas.

Holly Drummond (9)
The Mary Erskine & Stewart's Melville Junior School

Journey Through The Solar System

Magnificent magical Mercury,
See the stars that travel round thee.
Rusty red a rough colour,
Burning bashing causing a bother.

Venus the lovely goddess of love,
Another astronomer from above.
The planet she owns of course is the one
Circling second around the sun.

Earth events emerge early,
Pretty precise practically pearly.
Humans, some hate, some honour, some hug,
Some break a little, brittle bug.

The magical metallic planet Mars
Like a crashing crackling crater.
Red rusty and rocky landscape,
Leave the little planets till later.

Jumping in Jupiter gigantic and all,
A fearsome frightening nasty fall.
Fifth from the sun somewhere out there,
Jumping on Jupiter away out there.

Soaring Saturn and its stars,
Are many moons away from Mars.
Rings of red and stars of silk,
Smooth and white, as white as milk.

Uranus the unnecessary planet,
Revolves its rings round and round it.
Blue and green its general colours,
Whether the water has its wonders.

Noble Neptune never knows,
Which way to turn to warm his nose.
It's eight in line, its chilly face,
A long way out, in outer space.

Poor old Pluto's petrified,
It's dark and cold and iced inside.
The next galaxy is very close,
Is anyone out there? Nobody knows.

Jessica Findlay (9)
The Mary Erskine & Stewart's Melville Junior School

Favourite Food

One scrumptious chocolate cake
A delicious treat
On the top shelf of the fridge
For me to eat

Two tasty cheeseburgers
A delicious treat
In my bag from Burger King
For me to eat

Three sizzling sausages
A delicious treat
Spitting on the barbecue
For me to eat

Four yummy bananas
A delicious treat
Sitting in the fruit bowl
For me to eat

Five green apples
A delicious treat
Hanging outside on the tree
For me to eat.

Callum Airlie (8)
Westruther Primary School

Apples

Five scrummy apples
Ripening some more
Along came a hungry bear
And then there were four

Four yummy apples
Hanging on a tree
Along came a gust of wind
And then there were three

Three crunchy apples
Beneath the sky so blue
Along came a naughty goat
And then there were two

Two scrumptious apples
Looking rather yum
Along came a hurricane
And then there was one

One juicy apple
Sitting in the sun
Along came James
And then there were none!

James Conington (8)
Westruther Primary School

Seashells

Glittering all day
Lying on the golden sand
The calm shells shimmer
Home to mini animals
Keeping them safe from harm
Some cling to rocks
Holding on tight
Sparkling in the orange sun
A wonderful sight!

Elizabeth Wilson (8)
Westruther Primary School

My Dog

My dog is a sleek black lab,
His eyes glow like green rubies,
He never fusses when he gets a jab!
My dog is the best of all doggies.

Leaping up and down like a frog,
My faithful dog is a beautiful sight,
He's always delighted to go for a jog,
Though he barks at night.

He gobbles down his food in a flash
And he runs around like a cheetah,
So he doesn't scream when he has a gash,
My dog's the best even though he's hyper.

Drew Airlie (10)
Westruther Primary School

Rebbecca

Her dark eyes twinkled like shimmering stars,
Her sable coat glimmered in the sunshine,
I gazed at this enchanting pony,
Spellbound by her amazing beauty.

I reached out a trembling hand
To touch her velvety muzzle,
She blew softly on my ice-cold hand,
She stared at me contentedly,
I couldn't believe that she was mine,
Rebbecca, my new pony.

Suzan Reshad (11)
Westruther Primary School

The Dolphin

As the springy little dolphin
Entered the huge ring
He swam around the side
He jumped and curved
Like a half moon
People clapped like
Whales' tails against a hard rock
The dolphins on the other side
Giggle in their squeaky voices
They all
Bounce and dive and fly through the air
But how they do it
I cannot say!

Joanna Wilson (8)
Westruther Primary School

The Husky

Pulling the heavy sledge
Speedily, powerfully
Through the biting wind
Her fur is as soft as silk
Her eyes are as blue as the sky
Oh how much I wish for one
Of my own
To love, to cuddle
To be my favourite
Husky.

Holly Reshad (9)
Westruther Primary School

Izzy - My Pony

Trundling up the track,
The sound of ponies grazing,
Steel gates creaking open
Into luscious green pastures,
My enchanting chestnut
Fidgets impatiently in her horsebox,
My heart misses a beat,
My treasured possession and I
Are filled with anticipation,
She zooms from captivity,
Like a rocket in space,
She gleams spectacularly in the sunshine,
Her saddle is a sofa,
Smooth and soft,
The lesson commences,
Ponies dart and buck,
But my angel canters,
Undeterred,
Her dainty movements
Set an example,
She leaps over the jump amazingly,
Is she real?

Jennifer Smith (11)
Westruther Primary School

My Dogs

My dogs are tiny and woolly,
They look like balls of fluff,
They run around and chase the cars,
They like to prove they're tough!
My mum thinks they are funny,
They sure look kind of cute,
One of them is golden yellow,
The other wears a cool black suit,
Polly is the biggest,
KK's a little thin,
We're all off to Crufts this year
And are hoping for a win.

Oliver Muir (11)
Westruther Primary School

In The Jungle

Colours exploding the moment you enter
Humid air above the glittering river
I clamber, spellbound through the tangled creepers
Delicate blue butterflies fluttering around
I perch on a mossy branch, not noticing the snake
Entranced by the vivid flowers growing all around
A humming bird hovers just above my head
I'm amazed at the beauty in this enchanting world.

Kathleen Long (10)
Westruther Primary School

Friendship

A friend is someone who cares for you,
a friend is someone who shares with you.
A friend is someone who loves you,
a friend is someone who would buy clothes for you

But . . .

A bully is someone who punches you,
a bully is someone who steals lunches from you.
A bully is someone who nags you,
a bully is someone who nicks bags from you

But . . .

What happens if they move away?
I guess you will just sit on the bay.
Just crying to say, 'Oh please come back
Or my mum will get the sack'

But . . .

You would cheer if the bully's away
And be dying to say to your friends, 'He's away!'

Scott Kempik (9)
Whitdale Primary School

Buddies And Bullies

Caring and sharing is all around us
But many do not share or care
We like to share and care

Love is friendship
A good friend is someone who cares
A bad friend is a bully
A good friend is a good person

A bad friend is a bad person
A good friend is a loving person.

Harris Loureiro (9)
Whitdale Primary School

Good And Bad Side Of Friendship

Every day you should be happy
You can dress up cool too
Only bad people are bad

Everybody being supportive to other people
They would be helpful to you as well
Loving and caring is a good thing

Bad people would be nasty, grinning, greedy and spiteful
Good people would be funny, jolly, kind and sharing
Your family is important to you as well

Being greedy is not a good person
Being kind is a fantastic person
Being funky is like being a DJ.

Callum Millar (9)
Whitdale Primary School

Friends

Friends are nice
Friends will care
When you're feeling down
Friends will always share

Nobody likes bullies
Bullies are not nice
Bullies will take your dinner money
Bullies even have mice

Friends are there to help
Friends are there to share
Friends are helpful, kind and even share.

Eva Leslie (9)
Whitdale Primary School

What's A Buddy And A Bully

A friend is a buddy
They're caring and sharing
You don't know they might be a bit grubby

A bully is not nice
A bully could be scared
They could be scared of mice

A buddy is happy
They could be a bit old
They could have changed your nappy years ago

A bully is not nice
Or happy like a buddy
I think bullies don't like rice

A buddy is a friend
They will stay and play
Even to the end

A bully will pick on you
All day long
You can hear the tick tock clock and the bully behind.

Connor McGonigal (9)
Whitdale Primary School

Bad And Good

Tom moved house and school
Sarah-Jane is a bully
Sarah-Jane is unkind and nasty
Tom is kind, helpful, caring and loving
Tom looks at her thinking she's cool
Sarah-Jane is greedy and steals money
Sarah-Jane lies about people
Tom is sharing, caring and helps.

Sophie Renwick (9)
Whitdale Primary School

The Dark And Light Side Of Friendship

Friendship is when you have a friend
Friendship is loyal and true
Friendship is when you have a friend caring for you

Loyal and sharing friends will mean a lot to you
They *never* hurt you
Or *never* bully you (as some might do)

If you don't have a friend
You will get hurt and swore at
They're just nasty name-callers

Bullies constantly bicker at you
They think it makes you big and smart

When you have a friend you know
If you have one love and passion will grow.

April Penman (9)
Whitdale Primary School

The Good Side Of Friendship

Friendship is when you are kind
Friendship is when you are truthful
Friendship is when you are honest and nice
Friendship is when you are thoughtful

If you don't have friends you will have to be more kind
Friendship is all about caring and loving
Friendship is when you have lots of friends to play with

If you still don't have a friend
Give them their money back
Then you'll have lots of friends.

Andrew Easton (9)
Whitdale Primary School

The Good Side Of Friendship

Friendship is love
We need it every day
Caring and sharing
From all around us

Friendship is kind
Loving, caring, nice
We need it twice a day
It helps us to get around

Friendship is happy
It feels lovely
Good buddy
From all good people

Friendship is bad
But it helps people
It's also caring
It's feeling jolly

Friendship is family
That is lovely
It is sharing
Friends are funky

Friendship is nasty
It is bad to bully
Happy, caring, sharing
It gets you around places

Friendship is kindness
It always gets people happy
It is happy and caring
It is nice to be kind.

Aaron Brown (10)
Whitdale Primary School

The Friends

Friendship is
all about loving and caring.

Friendship is
all about talking and playing.

Friends are kind and
tell you all their secrets.

Friendship is
all about sharing.

Friendship is
all about believing and trusting.

Friendship will always
be there for you.

Friendship is
all about listening.

Friendship is
all about nice times.

Megan Brady (9)
Whitdale Primary School

A Friend Or A Bully

The happiness of friendship
Brings laughter to your door
Some people are not friends though
So these people hurt instead
These people are called bullies
They call you names and lie
A good friend wouldn't do this
They would play instead of push
Why do people do this?
There isn't a reason to
Everybody is the same on the inside
So why bully, push or lie?

Jonathan Hay (9)
Whitdale Primary School

The Difference Between Friends And Bullies

Friends are caring and nice
Bullies start big, huge fights
Friends help you if you're stuck
Bullies just be horrid and cruel

Buddies are sharing and kind
Bullies are greedy and they tease you
Friends are supportive and friendly
Bullies always dare people

Friends are jolly and funky
Bullies are nasty and bigger than you
Friends hang out with you
Friends play with you
Friends like you
Friends help you
Friends visit you.

Lauren Stewart (9)
Whitdale Primary School

My Puppy Dog Friend

We go somewhere
We take the mutt
I feel dog food stuck to my foot
She sneaks up the stair
Tries to jump in the bed
I fling her out the bed
She'll land on her head
When I bathe her she runs through the mud again.

Louise Walker (9)
Whitdale Primary School

Friends, Bullies And Family

Friends can come in all different ways
Happy, jolly, caring, sharing, kind, loving, helpful
And supportive every single day
We need our friends to make it through the day,
Week, month and year

Bullies are opposite of friends
They tease, are never helpful
And never ever kind
So the best thing to do is to stay away
And never get involved

Family is loving, caring, sharing, helpful and happy
Even though we argue with them
The bond will never break
An example is me and my sister
We're never finished arguing but no matter what
We'll always love each other.

Lauren Wilson (9)
Whitdale Primary School

School Is A Jail For Children

School is a jail for children
We sit for six hours a day
When mums and dads say
We should be outside to play

We sit with six hours of torture
With language and reading to do
If you were much younger and smarter
You'd probably know what to do

Whips and chains are sore but
Language and reading hurt more, please
I beg, I beg, please do not throw me
Out of the door.

Gareth Campbell (10)
Whitdale Primary School

Both Sides Of Friendship

The bullies were there today
I just sat there and laid
In pain and agony

When I went home
I fell and skinned my knee
Because of this my whole family
Surrounded me as I cried
They cuddled and kissed me

My family are very supportive
Not like the bully
He doesn't even want me to live
This is why I'm covered in bruises

My friends are as kind as can be
But the bully would rather break my knee
I feel so alone
As I sit here and sigh
I wonder why? Why? Why?

Tiffany Whiteford (9)
Whitdale Primary School

Our Holiday

This year my family and I are going to Spain
I get really excited until I reach the plane
I really hate flying
Sometimes I start crying
Then we've landed and I'm alright
Ready to enjoy my fortnight.

Rachel Cunningham (10)
Whitdale Primary School

Watching The Rain

There are two drops of rain
Sliding down the windowpane

Both of them have different names
One is Jane and the other is James

I'm going to see which one's the worst
That depends on who comes first

James has began to snooze
He is probably going to lose

Jane is going fast
So I don't think she'll come last

James is going at last
Jane is still going fast

James has just went by
Jane is about to cry

In the end James had won
Jane said she had no fun

That's the end of James and Jane
Sliding down the windowpane.

Tammy Dickson (10)
Whitdale Primary School

The Sleeping Tiger

Tiger, tiger in the night
He loves the night but he hates the light

He sleeps in the day and sleeps at night
He doesn't even wake to see the beautiful sight

He dreams all day
He yawns all night

Not even a herd of elephants
Could wake him from light or night.

Patrick Thornton (10)
Whitdale Primary School

Going To France

I have to find my suitcase,
I have to find my hat,
I have to find my board games,
Because I'm going to France.

I cannot find my suitcase,
I cannot find my hat,
I have to find them quickly,
Because I'm going to France

I must have looked too quickly,
I must have looked too fast,
Because now I'm falling down the stairs,
I hope I'm going to France.

I wake up and my mum is holding
An ice-pack on my head,
She said I've got concussion and
We're staying home instead.

Aimee Douglas (10)
Whitdale Primary School

My Best Friend, Teila

My dog was funny
Because she jumped like a bunny.
She chased her tail
As she drank her ale.
She was the best
Although she was a little pest.
Teila was big-eared
But other dogs never feared.
In doggy years she was seven
But now my Teila's asleep up in Heaven.

Vicky Christie (10)
Whitdale Primary School

My Perfect Year

Wintry January starts a 'Happy New Year'
We play in the snow and laugh and cheer

In February, while skiing I numb my tiny toes
And old Jack Frost he nips my frozen nose

The wild winds arrive in March
They blow me over when my feet they catch

As the month of April comes into sight
I love how the buds and spring become alight

When the new spring lambs are born in May
I smile at their cute and cuddly ways

I really love the arrival of June
For it means the holidays will be here soon

In July it is my birthday, a very special day
My friends and family appear - 'Happy Birthday' they all say

August means back to school
I have to work hard so I won't be a fool!

September means summer will soon be forgotten
The leaves are changing, it will soon be autumn

In October at Hallowe'en I get scared
With monsters and witches creeping everywhere

I like to be outside on the fifth of November
Fireworks and bonfires are a thing to remember

December announces the end of the year
'Merry Christmas' brings friends and families near.

Sarah McNeill (10)
Whitdale Primary School

I Wonder Why?

I was sitting in my room,
Wondering,
Why o' why
Are there
Cats and rats
And dare I say,
. . . Bbbbbats?
Who made all of these creepy things and why?

What are stars?
Are they Mars bars?
God, God,
That's what they're always telling me
Who is He?
Why is He so important?
He created the world,
The stars and all,
The universe you may say!

I wonder why
Birds fly
And kids cry?
I wonder why
Why o' why?

Jasmyn Leigh Crowden (9)
Whitdale Primary School

The Fierce Bat Poem

There was a bat
Who lived in the dark
In a hole in a tree
He likes living there
So he can sit and stare
But he is fierce

He is a fierce bat
He is worse than a cat
He tries to do bad things to other bats
It is so bad
They feel sad

So one night
His eyes were light
He went to fly and see the other bats
He saw them and started flying into them
They were all sad and hurt
Then he didn't like it to see bats being hurt anymore
So he didn't do it anymore.

Claire Longridge (10)
Whitdale Primary School

Summer Surprise

On a warm, misty evening,
With a distant sunset,
Lay the wondrous and pleasant meadows,
Looking bright with their different shades of yellows.

Then suddenly out of the blue,
Came a gleaming champion steed,
Galloping softly and swiftly,
Over the countryside splendour.

It was a wonderful sight to see,
On that beautiful summer's eve,
As we stood there and watched,
My brother and me.

Aimee McMahon (10)
Whitdale Primary School

My Little Sister

My little sister
She is good one day
And bad the next
She gets me into trouble
And she fights with me every day and night
She comes into my room in the morning and says, 'Get up'
She gives me kisses in the morning and at night
When my dad comes home from work she goes mad
And when he goes, she is sad
My little sister might be bad but I still love her no matter what!

Jade Ford (10)
Whitdale Primary School

The Vikings

Here they come,
the warriors in a fierce-looking boat
with a red and white sail.
Shields all around the side of the boat,
it's sailing towards us.
Hide, quick they're coming!
They're destroying our land,
hide what we have left.
The Vikings killed our people,
plundered our homes and villages.
They stole our precious books and things we worship.

Caitlin Stone (8)
Whitdale Primary School

Mysterious Invaders

They came in a boat from the north
Dressed in armour from head to toe
Our boat travels very swiftly in hail or snow
They are very, very vicious so you better beware
Wherever there is trouble the Vikings will be there

They invaded our country in 793
They are very scary men and very hairy
I'd really hate to tell
They are not the type of people that I would like to be

The monks are praying with faith and peace
When suddenly appears a boat
A dragon head on the prow
And the monks don't know . . .

Suddenly they jumped out their boat
And yelled, 'Here come the Vikings'
They attacked our monasteries
No longer there was peace
And the monks run so fast, the killing never ceases

Soon they left and they came back
Finally settling here
Peaceful settlers.

Jason Cleland (8)
Whitdale Primary School

The Vikings

V icious Viking warriors
I nvaded Lindisfarne
K illing people and animals
I nvading with helmets, shields and mighty swords
N asty adventures
G od and Lord help me please.

Jemma White (8)
Whitdale Primary School

The Vikings

We come on our voyages over the sea
To find new settlements
It is too rocky where we come from
We want gold, silver and precious books
We plunder and loot precious things
And goods to take home to eat
We take some slaves to sell
We are on our way to Lindisfarne
And we are called
The Vikings.

Alistair Brown (8)
Whitdale Primary School

The Vikings

The Vikings are coming to get our precious gold
And our books,
They travelled in a longboat
To burn our houses,
The boat had a dragon's head on the prow
to frighten all the monks away.

Kirsty Jack (8)
Whitdale Primary School

The Vikings

The Vikings are coming in a boat
And they're heading this way
So we better pack up our things
And leave the village
But where are we going to go?

Lauren Kerr (9)
Whitdale Primary School

The Vikings

They came on longboats to Lindisfarne
To take precious goods
They took cups and gold and our precious books
We fought for our god and died

They murdered the monks
Made the rest slaves

They found America

Settled here
Said they were brave.

Sarah Cochrane (8)
Whitdale Primary School

The Vikings

The Vikings are coming
So beware out there
So be on your guard
For they will strike you down
So run, run you men
Hide wherever you can
Watch your back
So you don't fall over.

Debbie Cuthbert (8)
Whitdale Primary School

The Vikings

V icious Vikings
I ndestructible, strong
K illing, looting, plundering
I nvaders, warriors
N asty adventures
G ods like Thor, the thunder god.

Lauren Bonnar & Heather Weir (8)
Whitdale Primary School

Vikings

The Vikings came from the north
in their fierce boats heading to Lindisfarne.
The monks were peaceful
and didn't do any harm to anyone.
The Vikings came armed with swords,
shields and spears.
The Viking ship had a dragon's head on the prow,
it was there to scare enemies.

Jack Compton (8)
Whitdale Primary School

The Vikings

The Vikings have invaded our country
they stole our precious books.

They burned our church and killed many people
and all just for fun.

They took our gold and sailed back home
leaving our home a wreck.

Lewis Perry (8)
Whitdale Primary School

Vikings

V icious Vikings killing.
I nvade the monks.
K illing people.
I ntruders.
N asty Vikings.
G od Thor.

Ryan Douglas (8)
Whitdale Primary School

The Vikings

They came from the north,
They were warriors and invaders.
They went to Lindisfarne and killed the monks,
They invaded Britain and discovered America,
They were good farmers and soldiers.

Darcey O'Rourke (8)
Whitdale Primary School

Night Sky

His hair is like the sharpest star
His face is a full moon
His heart thumps like thunder
He is the night sky

The leaves follow him like a shadow
He makes the wind blow hard
He makes people wish he wasn't there
He is the night sky

He's a horrible hated horror
He's the king of the night sky
He's as fierce as a lion
He is the night sky.

Allan Thomson (11)
Woodburn Primary School

Rainforest Night

The eyes are only visible to the bodies that disappear,
Those wonderful unblinking eyes mingle in with fear.
They make me want to run, but I'm rooted to the spot,
A scream fills the air and I don't have any thought.
Flying through the forest with the power of a jet,
Now I know that all my fears fully have been met.
I jump and hide in thick branch seating,
As I hear those creatures eating.
I pray to God I'm not the main course,
As the creature bit with dreadful force.
A night in the forest is like horror in a house,
Everything seems to be as quiet as a mouse.
Now you know that no one's there,
Behind any tree to give you a scare.
As you relax you know nothing's there,
Except those eyes that forever stare.

Ryan Dempster (11)
Woodburn Primary School

Summer

In summer we get time off school,
To go and play in the pool,
On a hot summer's day,
I go out to play.

I try to play volleyball,
But I'm too small.
While I'm out horse riding,
My sister is at the park sliding.

It is very, very hot
That I need a lollipop.
Summer is nearly finished,
Autumn is coming soon.

Alisha Allen (11)
Woodburn Primary School

Blank!

At the blank piece of paper I sit and stare,
I look for inspiration, but find none there.
Thoughts keep flying through my head,
Then I realise my mind is dead.

I look around at all my friends,
Suddenly my imagination ends.
They're all scribbling merrily away,
They're going to be finished by the end of the day.

I can't think of anything smart,
They tell me poems should come from the heart,
I'm in such an awful state,
It'll not be finished next year at this rate!

Samantha Howie (11)
Woodburn Primary School

The Rainforest Woman

I look ahead to see an exquisite woman,
Her hair is as long as Liana's,
Her face pretty as the sunrise,
Her long flowing arms reaching for forest which is not there,
Her long slim body like a tree trunk,
I wish I was her standing there on her own,
She has no worries, no fears, nothing on her mind,
She's free like a bird,
I open my eyes and I see a man,
He is standing there with her holding her hand,
But now they are together forever,
Now I open my eyes to realise that it was all a dream.

Sammi Kelly (11)
Woodburn Primary School

One Gentle Night

He is the night
The dark silence across the land
He is the night
A manly shape in the sparkling sky

The night is he
On the shadowed hillside
The night is he
Across the mountain tops

He is the night
Darkening the window-lit houses
He is the night
Sparkling with the bright stars

The night is he
Blackening the thick forests
The night is he
Floating in the river's reflection

He is the night
Gloomily from twilight
The night is he
Until the morning sunlight.

Laura Haining (11)
Woodburn Primary School

My Fighter Brother

My fighter brother
is an active one
fighting and biting
those crystal-blue eyes

That cute little smile
he bolts and darts
smashing glass and hiding
shouting and screaming

Throwing and shooting
punching and kicking
and at night
he snuggles up
in my arms
and falls into
a deep sleep.

Paul Hart (11)
Woodburn Primary School

Night Poem

As he glides through the air the brown crispy leaves
Follow him
Step by step the leaves glide with him
He loves to whistle every night
He whistles like a newborn bird
Calling for its mother
His smile is like a beautiful moon
His clothes are made of leaves and branches
His face looks like every beautiful thing in the world.

William Baxter (11)
Woodburn Primary School

Darkness

The waves crashing against the rocks
The whistling wind whisking around
The rain trickling down the mountain
There she stands on the mountaintop high
Lucy

The big creamy moon gleaming brightly
Harsh thunder cries loudly
The lightning illuminates the sky
There she stands on the mountaintop high
Lucy

The hooting owls rattling the leaves
The howling wolves and foxes
The creepy badgers creeping by
There she stands on the mountaintop high
Lucy

The clock in town strikes midnight
The gate rapidly banging
Spirits dancing round and round
There she stands on the mountaintop high
Lucy

The thunder breaks harsher
Bats flying about
The Earth begins to shake
That's something that scares Lucy.

Iesha Steele (11)
Woodburn Primary School

The Eagle

Swooping from a very high place
The eagle starts to show his face
Soaring down to slowly catch his prey
And that's his meal for the rest of the day

After his meal he gets some rest
For the eagle has done his best
On this peaceful silent night
In a couple of hours there will be light

It is morning and the eagle awakes
Before it goes hunting he takes a break
He stands up to see the weather
He turns around and plucks a loose feather

Then the eagle flies away
To another destination for the day
People love these magnificent beasts
For most of them come from the east.

Dean Watson (11)
Woodburn Primary School